Poverty
and
Inequality
The Political Economy
of
Redistribution

Jon Neill
Editor

1997

W.E. Upjohn Institute for Employment Research
Kalamazoo, Michigan

Library of Congress Cataloging-in-Publication Data

Poverty and inequality : the political economy of redistribution / Jon
Neill, editor.
   p. cm.
   Includes bibliographical references and index.
   ISBN 0-88099-182-8 (alk. paper), — ISBN 0-88099-181-X (pbk. :
alk. paper)
   1. Poverty—United States—Congresses. 2. Income distribution—
United States—Congresses. 3. Transfer payments—United States—
Congresses. I. Neill, Jon (Jon Raymond)
   HC110.P6P593   1997
   362.5 ' 0973—dc21   97–32412
                                                                          CIP

Copyright © 1997
W. E. Upjohn Institute for Employment Research
300 S. Westnedge Avenue
Kalamazoo, Michigan 49007–4686

Cover design by J. R. Underhill
Index prepared by Leoni Z. McVey.
Printed in the United States of America.

Preface

The papers in this volume are based on the lectures delivered in the 31st Annual Lecture-Seminar Series of the Department of Economics at Western Michigan University. The title of that series was "The Economics of Rich and Poor: The Political Economy of Income Redistribution."

This series was organized by the Lecture-Seminar Series Committee whose members were Jon Neill (Chair), Kevin Hollenbeck, William Kern, and Paul Thistle.

The Department of Economics gratefully acknowledges the financial and moral support of the W.E. Upjohn Institute for Employment Research, which has been a co-sponsor of this series for the past 15 years.

Jon Neill
Kalamazoo, Michigan
September 1997

CONTENTS

Introduction

Jon Neill
Western Michigan University

In the early 1970s, the War on Poverty appeared to be near a successful conclusion. In 1960, 18.1 percent of American families were living in poverty. But by 1973, the poverty rate of American families had fallen to 8.8 percent. Over this thirteen-year period there was an equally impressive reduction in the percentage of families living near poverty. The percentage of families below 125 percent of the poverty level dropped from 25 to 12.8 percent. During the 1960s, inequality also declined significantly, at least by some measures. In 1960, the top quintile of families earned 41.3 percent of aggregate income while the bottom quintile earned 4.8 percent, for a ratio of income shares of 8.6. By 1970, this ratio had fallen to 7.57.

Unfortunately, the success of the U.S. economy in reducing poverty and inequality did not continue into the next decade. After 1973 the poverty rate rose fitfully, to 10.3 percent in 1980, 10.7 percent in 1990, and 11.7 percent in 1992. Likewise, the near-poverty rate climbed 3 percentage points, to 15.8 percent. Changes in the shares of aggregate income received by families at the top and bottom of the income distribution were no less disturbing. Between 1970 and 1980, the top to bottom quintile share ratio rose slightly, to 7.98. However, over the next ten years it increased dramatically, to 10.14. In fact, each of the first four quintiles earned a smaller fraction of aggregate income in 1992 than they did in 1980. In total, there was a transfer of 3.1 percent of aggregate income from these four quintiles to the top quintile, with about 74 percent of this transfer going to families in the top 5 percent of the income distribution.[1]

In looking for an explanation for this trend, it is perhaps tempting to turn to changing political and social conditions and institutions. Yet while political and social change may have played an important role in reshaping the distribution of income in the United States, income distribution is ultimately an economic phenomenon. After all, income is determined by market forces and the policies that governments adopt to restrain and redirect them. Without a thorough study of the economic events of the past twenty years, it is highly unlikely that this unsettling rise in poverty and inequality can be fully understood.

To answer the questions that these unhappy events confront us with, it is necessary to consult economists from a fairly wide range of fields. To begin with, the distributional changes of the past decade and a half must be carefully quantified and placed in the proper context. For example, it is important to know if these changes were confined to particular regions or subgroups in the United States, and if they were reflective of changes taking place in other industrialized economies. International trade has become a much larger part of economic life, and the U.S. economy is no longer a monolith, largely unmoved by economic developments abroad.

The role of the political process in determining the distribution of income would also seem to be of paramount importance. Although it may be coincidental, the rhetoric and policies of the Reagan-Bush administration constituted a clear repudiation of the social philosophy and programs of the Kennedy-Johnson administration. In any case, one cannot help wondering how it is that, in a democratic society, the top 20 percent of the population would be able to increase its share of aggregate income. This is an interesting public choice question, but the failure of middle- and lower-income families to increase their share of aggregate income may be at least partly due to the intergenerational transmission of economic status.

However important these questions may be, many find the most interesting and provocative aspect of the disfavor which the economy has shown poor and middle income families over the past two decades to be the bounty that it simultaneously created for others. Although the economy did not grow as rapidly during the 1980s as it did during the 1960s, the decade was marked by impressive growth in real domestic product. Between 1982 and 1990, real GDP increased about 30 percent. But unlike other expansions, this one was not accompanied by less poverty and inequality; the benefits from the expanding economy apparently did not trickle down, as so many argued would happen.

Of course the relationship between growth and distribution is complicated and obscure. Presumably wages rise rapidly in an expanding economy, more rapidly than other components of income. And since poor and low-income families are typically families for whom wages are the most important component of income, many are pulled out of poverty and into the middle class by the expansion. Thus, the obvious question is: what role did labor markets play in reshaping the distribution of income? A quick look at the wage and salary component of national income reveals that, in real terms, there was only modest growth between 1980 and 1990, about 26 percent, compared to over 49 percent between 1960 and 1970. In fact, this component grew only slightly more than it did between 1970 and 1980 (22.5 percent), a period that is not usually viewed as a time when the economy was good to wage earners. Moreover, the share of national income generated by wages and salaries continued to decline. This share rose slightly more than 2 percentage points between 1960 and 1970, but fell almost 5 percentage points between 1970 and 1990.

The lecture series that produced the essays in this volume was organized for the purpose of bringing together six well-known economists to learn their views on these and related issues. The lectures were delivered at Western Michigan University during the 1994-95 academic year, at the height of the debate over the need for welfare reform. The points raised by the authors reflect the concerns and hopes of many economists for that endeavor. They also offer a perspective from which to observe and evaluate the impact of the recently passed Personal Responsibility and Work Opportunity Reconciliation Act on the behavior and economic fortunes of low income families.

The essay that opens this collection is by Professor Robert Haveman. What Professor Haveman offers us is a critique of the two proposals that shaped the current debate over welfare reform, the proposal from the Clinton Administration and that found in the Contract With America. It is not surprising that both plans emphasize moving welfare recipients off the welfare rolls and into the labor market, since this has been a long-playing theme in U.S. political economy. Even when the War on Poverty was at its height and a guaranteed income was being given serious consideration, many—including liberals such as Robert Kennedy—continued to maintain that finding jobs for the poor, or as Lyndon Johnson put it, turning "tax-eaters" into tax-payers, should be the purpose of the nation's welfare system.[2] However, Professor Haveman argues that the labor market today is markedly different from the labor market of the 1960s. Consequently, the prospects for moving significant numbers of people off the welfare rolls and into jobs paying wages that would lift them out of poverty may be more remote and, very likely, not particularly cost-efficient.

The next contribution to this volume is Professor Rebecca Blank's analysis of the relationship between the incidence of poverty and economic growth. It is often argued that the most effective policies for reducing poverty and inequality are pro-growth policies. The coincidence of rapid growth and a declining poverty rate throughout the 1960s would seem to support this relationship. Yet the 1980s presents a compelling counter-example. Professor Blank evaluates a number of explanatory hypotheses that have been offered, and like Haveman, she sees the labor market as problematic. In her opinion, skilled-biased technical progress and the internationalization of the U.S. economy may be the two major reasons for the failure of growth to reduce the poverty rate.

The third and fourth essays, those by Professors John Formby and Timothy Smeeding, address the question of how widespread the rise in poverty and inequality actually was. In his paper, Professor Formby examines the extent of inequality in various U.S. geographical regions over the past three decades using different measures of inequality and definitions of income. His analysis clearly shows that comparisons of regional income distributions are sensitive to the way in which income is defined, and that while regional income distributions are becoming more similar, this is due to both a decrease in inequality in the South and increased inequality in the Northeast and West. Professor Formby ends his paper with an evaluation of the effect of recent policy initiatives on standard measures of inequality.

In contrast, Smeeding's essay focuses on cross-country comparisons of income distributions. From the data that he presents, two facts emerge. First, the United States has more inequality than any other OECD country. Second, though the increase in inequality experienced by the United States during the 1980s was not an isolated event, only a few OECD countries had as large an increase in inequality. Furthermore, in eleven of the twenty-four countries in Smeeding's survey, there was no discernible increase in disposable income inequality. This suggests that the safety net in many countries was sufficiently strong to resist the impact of the structural changes that took place, or that pro-active policies were effective in preventing inequality from increasing.

The papers by Jere Behrman and Gordon Tullock both speak to the intergenerational dimension of income transfers, though from different perspectives for different ends. Professor Behrman is concerned with the effect of a family's economic status on that of its children. At issue are the principles that guide the intra-household allocation of resources and the claim that the children of high income parents tend to have high incomes themselves. Behrman contrasts the assumptions and implications of two competing models of intra-household resource allocation in the light of recent empirical work to provide insight into how strong the connection between parent and child incomes may be. And although his analysis leads to the conclusion that the economic status of a child's parents plays a large role in determining the child's income, Behrman is quick to emphasize that the importance of education should not be discounted.

The paper that closes this volume raises a number of elusive and disturbing questions. Professor Tullock begins his discussion by asking: what if redistribution has a depressing effect on growth? While it may be that the relationship between economic growth and redistributive policies is unclear, there are theoretical reasons to suspect a negative relationship. In Tullock's view, such a relationship presents ethical questions and may explain the apathy of lower-income households toward redistribution. In reminding us that when growth is affected by redistribution, the economic status of future generations must be considered before writing any normative prescription, Professor Tullock's observations are both provocative and insightful.

These six essays offer a wide perspective on poverty and inequality from a group of scholars who have made significant contributions to this important field of research. They certainly are worthwhile reading for anyone concerned about rising poverty and inequality. It is wishful to think that recent developments are aberrant, that soon poverty and inequality will begin to decline, particularly if government stays the pro-growth course. Thus, if poverty and inequality create the social pathologies that have become commonplace in the United States, as so many argue, a "kinder, gentler" America is not likely to become a reality until this pernicious trend is reversed.

NOTES

1. The statistics cited here come from various issues of the *Statistical Abstract of the United States.*

2. Moynihan (1973, pp. 61-63, 130-131).

Reference

Moynihan, Daniel P. 1973. *The Politics of a Guaranteed Income: The Nixon Administration and the Family Assistance Plan.* New York: Vintage Books.

Welfare Report—1996 Style
Will We Sacrifice the "Safety Net"?

Robert Haveman
University of Wisconsin-Madison

Why is it that we have welfare reform on our plate again? In my opinion, the reasons are neither cost or program growth, nor any notion that we have a "welfare crisis," irrespective of what either President Clinton or House of Representatives Speaker Newt Gingrich say. Moreover, there are no new or startling revelations of waste and inefficiency.

In part, we got into this debate again because President Clinton started it. The fact is that every President since 1970 has had a welfare reform plan save George Bush. But this pushes the issue back a step. Why has every President felt a need to place this issue on the nation's agenda? In part, all observers agree that current income support policy contains bad incentives and gives the wrong messages to recipients; moreover, it has failed to reduce poverty.

For two decades now, we have seen antipoverty expenditures rising, but poverty has not been reduced. Under these conditions, it is difficult to argue that the strategy is working, especially when people are impatient. Moreover, the system that we have in place now has visible adverse incentives and a bewildering, multi-program patchwork that leads to well-known examples of horizontal inequity—among states, between one- and two-parent families, and between the working and nonworking poor. It discourages work, encourages family breakup, and prohibits the accumulation of assets beyond a bare minimum.

However, beyond all of these reasons for why we are again enmeshed in this debate is a simple overriding fact. There now exists a fundamental gap between the objectives of welfare and related programs and the society's social and economic goals.

At their core, existing welfare programs seek to secure for the market income poor a level of after-tax, or disposable, income that exceeds some minimum standard. They do this by distributing direct cash payments and providing essential goods.

Citizens today, on the other hand, see something quite different from the simple need for income assistance when they think of the poor population. Contrary to when the welfare system was started, we now expect that able-bodied women with children should contribute to their own well-being through work. We have also come to believe that for able-bodied people, there should be some *quid pro quo* associated with the provision of income support. And, if those requiring help are not job-ready, some seem to believe in education and training, rather than direct cash support; others advocate temporary public help followed by a termination of assistance.

At an even more fundamental level than work behavior, nonpoor citizens today expect minimum standards of civil behavior and responsible lifestyle decisions by those who receive public support. They are offended by dependency, teen out-of-wedlock births, homelessness, drug abuse and crime—all of which they see prevalent among the welfare recipient population.

While the images may be colored by stereotypes and prejudice (these problems are also concentrated in the African-American and Hispanic populations), to a large slice of nonpoor Americans, many of those in the bottom tail of the distribution today are there because of irresponsible choices they have made: the choice to bear children out of wedlock as a teen, the choice not to complete high school, the decision to refuse minimum wage employment when it is available, the decision to abuse drugs and sell them, the willingness to run in gangs and to engage in crime and violence, often against other poor people. After all, the poor did not used to be like this. And while many may be willing to admit that economic and social factors, urban schools, and the barriers created by racial prejudice may make these choices a rational response to the options available, they nevertheless seem to conclude that these socially costly and destructive outcomes are the result of choices encouraged by the welfare system.

If this characterization is true, the questions that people ask today about the current welfare system become more understandable. If recipients are able to engage in productive activity, why don't we require work as a condition of providing cash and in-kind assistance? If they are unable to break into regular jobs because of a lack of training or a lack of child care or health support, why don't we encourage them—or force them—to get whatever jobs they can so that they can accumulate the work experience necessary to advance? If they are having additional children who can be supported only by taxpayer assistance, or if they are working off the books, or drug-dealing when they should be learning, or opting not to marry in order to sustain public payments, or not requiring their kids to go to school, why should we simply provide support without attempting to change these behaviors?

In short, changes in general social standards, changes in the characteristics and behavior of the poor and welfare recipients, and changes in our expectations of them have created doubts about the wisdom of the welfare system as we know it.

Some Background on Poverty and Welfare Policy

Before getting into the specifics of the welfare reform debate, this section of the chapter presents some basic facts on poverty and welfare. Table 1 provides an overview of antipoverty programs since 1970. The years in the table correspond to peaks in the business cycle (1989 and 1992 are included for completeness).

The first two columns of the table show the number of persons with market incomes below the poverty line before and after cash transfers. Although not shown, in 1960, 39.9 million people (22.2 percent of the population) had after-cash transfer income below the poverty line. By 1970, this number had fallen to 25.4 million (or 12.6 percent of the population). Some combination of economic expansion, demographic changes, increased coverage and generosity of the social security system, and the War on Poverty/Great Society programs caused this improvement. Since 1973, however, the poverty population has increased sharply. The gain from 1979 to 1989 is particularly distressing; the sustained period of economic growth from 1982 to 1990 failed to raise the economic position of the poorest among us. Contrary to earlier experience, this rising economic tide did not lift these boats, and as a result, the common belief in the antipoverty impacts of good macroeconomic performance has been shaken.

Columns 4 through 6 show federal expenditures on the largest cash or "near-cash" means-tested—or antipoverty—programs. Through these programs, the nation currently spends around 1 percent of GDP on families and individuals with incomes below the poverty line.

Table 1. Poverty Population and Real-Cash and Near-Cash Transfer Program Expenditures, Selected Years

Year	Number of pretax, pretransfer poor (1000s)	Persons in official poverty (1000s)	Percent of population in official poverty	AFDC benefits[b]	Food stamp benefits	SSI benefits[b]	Total benefits	EITC expenditures	Benefits as a percentage of GDP
1970	n.a.	25,420	12.6	$15,051	n.a.	$10,627	$25,678	n.a.	0.70
1973	n.a.	22,973	11.1	22,382	$7,186[a]	10,801	33,183	n.a.	0.78
1979	42,783	26,072	11.7	19,382	11,184	13,672	44,238	$3,966	0.92
1983	52,700	35,303	15.2	17,975	16,585	13,247	47,807	2,528	1.00
1989	49,052	31,534	12.8	18,120	13,760	16,640	48,520	7,462	0.82
1990	50,851	33,585	13.5	18,529	15,717	17,277	51,523	7,437	0.87
1991	54,679	35,708	14.2	19,319	18,463	18,520	56,302	9,689	0.96
1992	57,350	36,880	14.5	20,431	21,884	21,258	63,573	11,783	1.05

SOURCE: U.S. Congress (1993, pp. 678, 867, 1058, 1312-13, 1609); U.S. Bureau of the Census (1993a, p. xviii); Council of Economic Advisors (1994, table B-1, p. 268, table B-59, p. 335).

NOTE: Benefits in millions of 1992 dollars.

a. Includes administrative costs of the program in 1973.

b. Includes state and federal benefits.

The Aid to Families with Dependent Children (AFDC) program, commonly referred to as "welfare," is the largest antipoverty income support program directed at families with children. The overwhelming bulk of recipients are single mothers and their children. The real value of aggregate AFDC benefits peaked around 1973; over the next ten years, real AFDC expenditures fell by almost 20 percent. Over the same period, the number of persons in families with incomes below the poverty line increased by 54 percent. Real AFDC expenditures have edged up since 1983. About 14 million people receive AFDC benefits, and two-thirds of them are children. AFDC spending accounts for about 1 percent of the federal budget, and about 2-3 percent of the budgets of most states.

The decline in AFDC benefits has been more than offset, in the aggregate, by a rapid increase in expenditures on the food stamp program, the nation's only antipoverty program available to all of the poor. There has been modest growth in the combined value of AFDC and food stamps.

In addition to these cash or near-cash benefit programs, a number of additional federal programs have significant antipoverty components. These include the medicaid program, public housing or housing assistance, and the Head Start program.

Finally, in the next to last column, information on the earned income tax credit (EITC) is shown. The EITC is a refundable tax credit on earned income directed primarily toward low-income workers with children. It is a major antipoverty program administered on the tax side of the budget. While its cost was about $12 billion in 1992, by 1996, the EITC is expected to be the largest cash or near-cash program directed toward low-income families with children.

This constellation of existing tax and transfer measures represents an important contribution to improving the lives of the nation's most disadvantaged and to reducing the incidence of pretax and pretransfer poverty. The full set of programs existing in 1991 removed from poverty nearly 20 million of the 55 million pretax and pretransfer poor; without these programs, the nation would have had a poverty rate of 21.8 percent, but with them in place the actual poverty rate was 14 percent. Without the programs in place, it would have taken over $160 billion (in 1991 dollars) to close the poverty gap; with them, the remaining poverty gap stood at about $52 billion.

This synopsis of poverty and welfare programs provides the necessary background for any sensible discussion of reform. However, this discussion cannot ignore how the U.S. economy has been evolving over the past twenty years. The simple fact is that the erosion of labor market opportunities for people with low levels of education has placed an enormous strain on the nation's antipoverty programs.

The figures in table 2, which show median incomes of men and women by their level of educational attainment, reflect the serious increase in inequality in the American economy. More important, they show the deterioration at the bottom of the distribution, which has contributed to the growing gap among the rich and the poor. In 1973, the median male with one to three years of high school had about $24,000 in income (in 1989 dollars); by 1989 the median worker with the same level of education had only $14,439 in income. Note that while the fall in income has been enormous for those with little education—both male and female—it has been greater for men than for women. Even so, the income level of women remains well below that for men.

Table 2. Median Income of Persons 25 and Over, by Educational Attainment and Gender, Selected Years, 1989 Dollars

	Males			Females		
	High school		College	High school		College
Year	1 - 3 years	4 years	4+ years	1 - 3 years	4 years	4+ years
1967	$22,858	$26,894	$39,186	$7,574	$10,800	$19,205
1970	23,442	28,034	40,527	7,629	10,866	19,735
1973	24,079	30,252	41,065	7,920	11,087	19,667
1979	18,697	26,416	36,636	6,726	9,085	16,923
1983	15,138	21,932	35,188	6,531	9,326	18,427
1989	14,439	21,650	37,553	6,752	10,439	21,659

SOURCE: U.S. Bureau of the Census (1990), for 1967-1983 figures; U.S. Bureau of the Census (1991); for 1989 figures.

I now want to consider the merits and implications of the two "reform" plans offered: the Clinton administration proposal and the proposal contained in the "Contract with America," which has served as the basis for the legislation passed by the Congress and signed into law by President Clinton in 1996. Though the currency of either plan is certainly open to question, both are likely to be important reference points over the next several years during which the new legislation will be implemented.

The Clinton Welfare Reform Proposal: Making Work Pay

It is into this maelstrom of political and economic pressures that the Clinton administration strode, promising to "end welfare as we know it." But exactly what is this plan, and how effective is it likely to be?

President Clinton's proposal was designed to "make work pay" through an expanded EITC, supplemented by child care assistance and job training. Indeed, a large step toward attaining this goal had already been taken by the time the President announced the remainder of his welfare reform plan. A major expansion of the earned income tax credit had been part of the 1993 Omnibus Budget Reconciliation Act (OBRA93). By 1998 the program is projected to cost $24.5 billion, $7 billion of which is the result of the 1993 expansion. For taxpayers with incomes in the lower earnings range of the credit, the expanded EITC can be thought of as a well-targeted increase in the minimum wage, to $5.95 per hour for families with two or more children, from $4.25 an hour. The expanded credit will deliver benefits to more than six million working taxpayers with incomes below the poverty line, will close the poverty gap by $6.4 billion, and will raise the incomes of over one million taxpayers to a level above the poverty line.

The proposal of the Clinton administration was also designed to make parents responsible, in part through child support enforcement and requiring women who give birth to establish paternity in the hospital. It would make recipients experience "Workfare"—including education and training—through a signed contract between recipients and government. It would discourage teen motherhood, by forcing teen moms to either live with their parents or send the check to the parents. It would change the "culture" of the welfare office by transforming caseworkers from check writers to counselors assessing capabilities and work out a training/education plan designed to achieve independence.

Finally, the Clinton proposal would force recipients to leave welfare after some point; "two years and out" is its most popular manifestation. Those able to work will be forced to operate in a world in which income support is a temporary and transitional "help," a mechanism designed to enable people to get their lives in sufficient order to live independently, relying on the returns from their own efforts. When the time limit for support has been reached, recipients will be turned out to find their own way in the world of work, assisted by child care subsidies and, of course, health coverage as a part of the president's health care reform proposal; if they are unable to find work, the government will presumably guarantee them a low-paying public service job (or, in some descriptions of the program, subsidize the private sector for providing jobs). However, this provision would have applied only to young recipients—those born after 1971—and then only to those with children older than one year. And, recipients not able to find a private sector job would be allowed to keep their public service job indefinitely—if they play by the rules, continue to search for a job, and not decline a job if it is offered.

The analytical support of this plan by administration spokespeople was consistent. They did want to change the expectations of the poor and establish a new norm. They did want to threaten the loss of benefits, in part because of the change in expectations that will result. At the same time, they sought to make jobs and working more attractive through supplements, services, and training. Their presentations made it clear that they saw health care reform as prior to welfare reform.

How Does the Clinton Plan Stack Up?

How do these elements of the Clinton proposal fare, especially in light of our critique of current policy? First, in my view, the expansion of the EITC is an extremely important, effective measure; it increases the return to work for taxpayers with children and does so in a coherent manner within the structure of the personal income tax. It will reduce poverty, and it has the right incentives.

Increasing efforts to collect and assure child support and to routinize the collection system are also to be commended. However, those who have studied this possibility—and who are its biggest advocates—suggest that no more than a marginal increment in the available income support will accrue to most mothers now on welfare.

The provision for time-limited welfare, training and education through workfare, child and health care assistance, and a guaranteed public service job are, in my view, dangerous territory. While changing the rules and benefit structure of welfare programs to minimize the rewards available for dysfunctional behavior is one thing, effectively canceling income support is quite another.

The fact is that most current recipients lack the basic capabilities to work themselves out of poverty on their own, even if they were to work full time, full year at the wage rate that their education, experience, and health characteristics would command. Take a look at table 3. Women recipients of AFDC are not a picture of job readiness. Nearly one-half of their children are less than five years of age, nearly one-half of them are high school dropouts, and less than 10 percent are working at all.

Table 3. Characteristics of AFDC Caseload, 1979-1991

Characteristic	March 1979	1986	1991
Ages of children			
Under 3	18.9	21.0	24.8
3 to 5	17.5	21.1	21.4
6 to 11	33.0	32.4	32.6
12 and over	29.8	24.3	21.4
Education of mother			
8th grade or less[a]	18.2	11.9	11.2
1-3 years high school[a]	39.8	35.5	35.1
4 years high school[a]	36.0	42.9	40.7
Some college[a]	5.2	8.4	12.2
College graduate[a]	0.8	1.2	0.8
Unknown	47.8	59.7	49.9
Mother's employment status			
Full-time job	8.7	1.6	2.2
Part-time job	5.4	4.2	4.2
Cases with reported earnings	12.8	7.5	7.9

SOURCE: Committee on Ways and Means, *1993 Green Book*, pp. 696-97.
a. Percentage distribution among mothers whose educational attainment is known.

Figure 1, taken from a recent study by Gary Burtless at the Brookings Institution, gives a sense of what these women would be able to earn if left on their own in the regular labor market. The bottom two lines show what former recipients have earned after leaving welfare. The top line is the most revealing one. It shows the amount of earnings of women with the capabilities of those who are now welfare recipients, if they were to work full time, full year. This level of earnings would leave the bulk of these families below the poverty line, even assuming that they could find such full-time jobs, and moreover it fails to recognize that the bulk of them have children who would require child care assistance were these mothers to work such hours.

Figure 1. Actual and Predicted Earnings among Women Who Received AFDC in 1979-1982

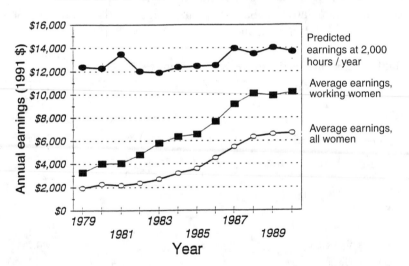

SOURCE: *The Work Alternative*, Nightengale and Haveman, eds., p. 84, Washington, D.C.: Urban Institute Press (1995). Used with permission.

While numerous training or welfare-to-work programs appear to pass a benefit-cost test, it is but a dream that the sort of training and remedial education that will be offered through "workfare" will make these people job-ready and economically independent. Moreover, the total costs of operating a reasonable public service jobs program are sufficiently high—in the neighborhood of $12,000 to $15,000 per worker per year—that current budgetary constraints insure that the demand for slots would far exceed the supply.

The "Contract with America"—Another Approach

Not long after the announcement of the Clinton plan, the midterm elections of 1994 were held, and both houses of Congress changed from being controlled by the Democrats to being controlled by the Republicans. The new majority party had run on a multipronged platform, called the "Contract with America," which included a welfare reform proposal.

The Republican approach to welfare was quite different from any that had been suggested heretofore. Although its specifics became modified in the process of congressional debate, its basic approach remained constant. In particular, the congressional proposal would:

- Turn over to the states—in the form of "block grants"— the funding for welfare (AFDC) that the federal government had been providing (less some amount to reflect expected efficiencies) and allow the states to do whatever they wanted with poor people in their jurisdictions. Moreover, the amount handed over would be kept constant for five years. As a result of this, poor people in various categories would no longer be entitled to support.

- Along with the "block grants," the federal government would impose a variety of constraints on how the states could use the money. In particular, they:
  - could not provide benefits to teenaged nonmarried mothers.
  - could not provide an increase in support to mothers who had another child.
  - could not provide support to either legal or illegal immigrants, with a few exceptions.
  - would deny benefits for life to any child who was born to an unmarried mother who gave birth while a recipient.
  - would beef up child support enforcement, much along the lines of the Clinton proposal.

- would impose a 60-month (or 5-year) cumulative limit on the time that recipients could secure support from the state program. Unlike the Clinton program, this limit would not be accompanied by support for education, training, child care, or public jobs once the time limit was encountered.
- would cut back on funding for other programs helping low-income people, such as food stamps, medicaid, and Head Start, and would seek to scale back the EITC.

How Does the "Contract" Stack Up?

Clearly, this congressional approach begins from a quite different and far more harsh view of the safety net programs in place in this country designed to help the least well-off among us. While one might view this harsh stance as sending a lesson regarding self-sufficiency and responsibility to adults who are recipients, it will inevitably carry adverse consequences for their children. Moreover, because the bulk of the people who will be affected by these harsh measures are African-American or Hispanic, the impacts of these measures across racial boundaries, may be quite unequal.

A variety of other concerns are also relevant in assessing this approach. First, some of the specifics of the program appear to be based on simple ideology, apart from any research knowledge or facts. For example, there is simply no evidence that the current system, which increases support along with family size, has encouraged additional births among the recipient population. One would be hard pressed to find a reputable researcher advocating the opposite position. Second, the notion that there is substantial money that can be saved seems to rest on a hope, rather than evidence. There is simply no evidence suggesting that efficiencies of the amount claimed are available to any new administrative procedure, whether state-based or not. Third, the constitutionality of the measures as they pertain to legal immigrants is an open question. These people, after all, are required to pay taxes, and are drafted into the nation's military when additional personnel are required. Finally, by failing to provide support for training, education, child care and job search—and by not requiring work-related efforts while receiving benefits, the "Contract" proposals seem weaker on work than does the Clinton plan.

This discussion leaves an overriding question regarding the longer term impact of the measures in the "Contract": What will happen to those recipients and their families who lose their benefits? While no one really knows, if I were pushed into a corner I would speculate that 10 to 15 percent of them would make a successful transition into the world of work and become self-sufficient, but at a low level. Another 70 percent or so would "cope"—they and their children would be severely disadvantaged, but they would adjust by combining households or moving in with relatives, or they would work some in intermittent and informal jobs. They would be poorer and even less capable of nurturing their children, but we wouldn't be vividly confronted by their hardships. We would only see the effects on their children a decade or two down the road. The remainder—say, 10 to 15 percent of those losing benefits—would become truly destitute. The effects on them would be obvious; homelessness would be only the most visible effect. The stock of recipients who now face benefit cutoff because of a five-year rule is about 1 million; 10 to 15 percent of this number is about 100,000 to 150,000. On average, each of these recipients has two children; hence, we are considering 300,000 to 450,000 people who would be visibly destitute. Surely, some of these would find their way onto the rolls of the Supplemental Security Income program—at federal government expense—or into the foster care system, at state and local expense.

Yet, it is the basic approach of this stern "Contract with America" proposal that is reflected in the new legislation passed by Congress, and signed—albeit reluctantly—by President Clinton. While some of the "Contract's" harsh edges have been sanded down, the entitlement of welfare has been eroded, block grants to states provided, work mandated, and prohibitions on assistance to various groups imposed.

Is the Real Problem "The Welfare System," or Is It the Collapse of the Bottom End of the Labor Market?

Unless I am wrong, the most critical problem of both the Clinton proposal and the Contract with America is their common presumption that the least able groups of the nation's working-age population can be successfully coerced into that niche of the labor market that has performed most poorly. As I have already noted, the low-wage sector is already struggling to absorb a large and growing flow of immigrants, both legal and illegal, as well as a rapid increase in female labor force participants, many of whom have few skills and little experience. If ever there was "swimming against the tide," this is it.

It is my strong judgment that these plans fail to address adequately the damper that the low end of the labor market places on opportunities for low-educated workers. The implicit assumption seems to be that the low-wage labor market can, without major dislocation, absorb up to two million additional low-skilled welfare recipients over the next few years. I have serious doubts that this is possible.

I would urge readers to note that there are interesting, high-potential policy ideas available for both increasing the private demand for low-skill labor and making these low-paying jobs more attractive. I am chagrined that neither the administration nor the Republican Congress has paid more attention to the potential of some of these options.

After all, numerous possibilities have been studied, and some have come away with rather high marks. One possibility would be a program modeled after the New Jobs Tax Credit, a measure that we actually had in place in the 1970s. The NJTC offers a tax credit in the range of $4,000 to $7,000 to employers who increase their employment level over some base level in the previous year. Because the credit is a flat amount, it forms a higher percentage in the wage bill for less-skilled workers than for more highly paid workers. It tilts the hiring decision towards lowest-wage workers.

Observers are convinced that a nontrivial increase in job creation for low-skill workers can be generated through this arrangement at a rather low cost to the Treasury, especially if the program is taken seriously, and publicized and administered efficiently. I would note that I am referring here to a universal program and not to the targeted jobs tax credit program.

A second possibility, this time on the supply side of the market, would be a wage rate subsidy. This program would complement an expanded EITC and make work pay even more directly. In this plan, a target wage rate, assume, say $10 an hour, would be set. Any worker taking a job at less than this amount, say $6 an hour, would be subsidized at a rate equal to 50 percent of the difference between the actual wage of $6 and the $10 target. Take-home pay would be $8 in this example: the $6 per hour market wage and the $2 wage rate subsidy. The effect of the plan would be to simply and effectively give low-wage workers, all low-wage workers, a labor-market advantage. It would make regular private sector work at low wages more attractive than it is now. Again, a number of potential concerns would have to be worked out, and the effects of the measure on the overall level of the market wage would have to be monitored.

The combination of this pair of employment incentives would improve the operation of the low-skilled labor market by generating ongoing demand- and supply-side pressure for the creation of jobs for marginal workers at reasonable cost. As such, it would equalize employment opportunities. By targeting the additional employment on underutilized segments of the labor market, national income could be increased without significant inflationary pressure. The combination will fundamentally alter the wage structure in private labor markets, raising the take-home pay of low-skilled workers relative to those with more secure positions in the labor market. The cost of an employment subsidy arrangement such as this would be substantially lower than providing equivalent jobs through public service employment, and lower still than dealing with the aftermath of the drastic cutbacks envisioned by the "Contract with America." Surely these suggestions should not be excluded from any serious national debate on poverty and poverty policy.

A Few Final Reflections

Let me conclude with a few final reflections on poverty and welfare in the United States today.

My first reflection is that welfare reform policy is no longer antipoverty policy. No longer do observers emphasize that the ultimate goal of all of this activity is to make the lives of poor people better than they are now. Getting people to work is equated with making their lives better; perhaps this might happen in the long run, but for sure, not in the short term.

A second reflection concerns institutions that no longer work in American society, and difficulty of government in replacing them. I have been struck by the enormity of the task of replacing families, churches, and neighborhoods by government. I am struck by how difficult and expensive it is to bring a young person, a child, to a position in which "work will work." Perhaps there is a lesson in our own personal experience that would be of use to government. How do we do it for our kids? Well, first we give them lots of education with monitoring and advice and expectations and parental participation in schools. Then, when they finish their schooling, we support them for a time while they get their heads together. Sometimes they engage in job search, sometimes they ski, sometimes they travel. Following this, we actively and in a one-on-one relationship, help them with job search. We help them prepare a resume, we put them into touch with friends and acquaintances, we help them to prepare for job interviews—all so they can find their own special niche in the world of work. Finally, we often support them in moving to another location, often far from our home if that is where the best opportunity for them is.

The main lesson, I fear, is that doing this effectively is costly, very costly. There is simply no way to do it on the cheap. The realization of this truth makes more distressing our talk of making welfare recipients self-sufficient with a reform that will at the same time save resources devoted to low-income families and their children.

A third reflection also relates to changes in the institutions that support and nurture the young. Like many other social scientists, I too am distressed by the growing incidence of out-of-wedlock births. But I am no less distressed by the Draconian measures regarding it often advocated by observers such as Charles Murray. There are, it seems to me, few good options here. There is moral suasion; there is denial of benefits; there is the requirement that teen mothers stay with their parents, perhaps frequently in a relationship that neither parents nor children will find productive; or there is keeping going as we are. Nothing looks very good, yet doing nothing seems wrong as well. I am simply troubled by what appears to be a near total lacunae concerning what appropriate and effective policy in this area might be.

In summary then, any cogent debate of welfare policy must begin with the recognition that a new economic, social, and ethical order is in place. This reality would seem to rule out certain options—such as a negative income tax—despite their theoretical and practical appeal. However, the mandating of work for millions of low-skilled people in a labor market environment in which relative demands and wage rates are falling seems unworkable, though consistent with the new reality. If this is ultimately what "welfare reform" is all about, an increase in poverty will be the result, and the next generation will experience all of the correlates of "growing up poor." If welfare reform reflecting this new reality takes the form of such work mandates, measures designed to improve the performance of the low-skill labor market would seem to be a necessary and natural complement.

Why Has Economic Growth Been Such an Ineffective Tool Against Poverty in Recent Years?

Rebecca M. Blank
Northwestern University

In the 1960s, the U.S. economy was flying high. Between 1961 and 1969, we experienced the longest and strongest economic expansion in U.S. history. The economy grew by an average of 4.3 percent per year, while unemployment was at 3.5 percent by the end of the decade. At the same time, the share of the population below the poverty line fell 9 percentage points, from 22 percent in 1960 to 13 percent by 1970.[1] Most economic analyses indicate that it was the booming economic growth that reduced poverty in the 1960s.

Now fast-forward to the 1980s. After two back-to-back recessions during 1980 and 1982, there was a strong and rapid recovery. From 1983 through 1989, the U.S. economy experienced its second longest and strongest expansion, topped only by the 1960s. Economic growth during these years averaged 3.7 percent per year. Unemployment fell from over 10 percent in December 1982 to slightly over 5 percent by 1989. But the poverty rate, which was over 15 percent at the beginning of the expansion of the 1980s fell only modestly. By 1990, after six years of economic expansion, it had declined only 2.4 percentage points and was still above its level of a decade before.

Now move forward again into the 1990s. A mild recession in 1990-1991 was followed by strong aggregate growth in 1992-1993. Not surprisingly, poverty rates rose in 1990-1991. Very surprisingly, poverty continued to rise in 1992-1993. The poverty rate, 15.1 percent, was very near where it was in 1983 at the end of a sharp steep recession. For the first time in modern U.S. economic history, economic expansion was associated with *increases* in the share of poor persons in the population.

This paper is about what happened over these years that caused economic growth to decline as an effective antipoverty tool. The first part compares the expansions of the 1960s and the 1980s and indicates why economic growth had far less effect on the income distribution in the 1980s than two decades earlier. We will discover that the primary culprit is a change in the demand for less-skilled labor that has driven down wages among less-skilled workers. The second section discusses some of the reasons for these labor market changes, and the third section discusses their political and policy implications.

The Death of "Trickle Down Economics"

It has been an axiom of public policy and political rhetoric that economic growth helps the poor. More than one president has claimed that "the best thing we can do for the poor is to make the economy grow." This strategy, often referred to as "trickle down economics," is extremely attractive, because it promises that we can fight poverty without substantial costs. Economic growth is expected to make middle-income Americans better off *at the same time as* it decreases poverty. This is a win-win solution to poverty, requiring no higher taxes on one group in order to redistribute to another. Unfortunately, this solution has been largely ineffective over the past fifteen years.

Figure 1 shows both the poverty rate and the size of the overall economy as measured by Gross Domestic Product (GDP), the most frequently used measure of overall economic capacity, from 1960 to 1993.[2] Between 1961 and 1969, the U.S. economy experienced its longest economic boom, as can be seen from the steep upward rise in GDP. Poverty fell 9 percentage points during that period. Between 1983 and 1989, the U.S. economy experienced its second-longest expansion. Poverty declined only 2.4 percentage points during that period, and remained well above its historic low of 11.1 percent in 1973. This is reinforced in the 1990s, when strong economic growth is associated with *increases* in poverty.

One measure of how surprising these changes are can be seen by going back to an economics article published in the mid-1980s by Alan Blinder and myself (Blank and Blinder 1986). In that article, we estimated the relationship between macroeconomic indicators and the overall poverty rate. Using data from 1959 (when official poverty numbers begin) to 1983, we were able to track poverty based on the core unemployment rate, the inflation rate, the share of government transfers to the poor, and several other macroeconomic indicators. We can use that historical relationship between the macro economy and poverty to predict the poverty rate over the 1980s, based on what actually happened in the macro economy. Our evidence would have predicted that by 1989 the poverty rate should have been down to 9.3 percent, driven by declining unemployment and low inflation. In reality, the actual poverty rate was 12.8 percent, much higher.[3]

Figure 1. U.S. Poverty Rate vs. Gross Domestic Product

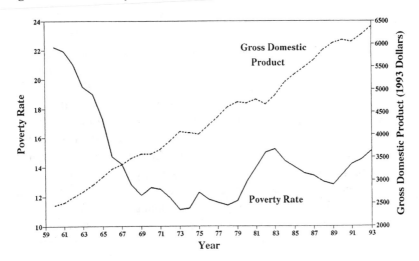

This exercise provides clear evidence of two things: First, no economist should be so foolish as to engage in economic predictions. Second, the historical relationship between macroeconomic growth and changes in poverty has fundamentally deteriorated.

Over the past five years, I have been involved in several research projects, exploring these changes in the relationship between economic growth and poverty.[4] Let me first indicate what the causes of the sluggish decline in poverty are *not*. While the following stories are often told, they turn out not to explain what is happening:

1. The problem is *not* that we are mismeasuring poverty in the 1980s and 1990s. Poverty rates are based only on cash income and do not consider what we call "in-kind" transfers. In-kind transfers include noncash public assistance programs, such as food stamps or housing assistance. While it is true that in-kind transfers have expanded among the poor, most of this expansion occurred in the 1970s, when such programs were increasing rapidly. Poverty rates that include in-kind income decline by almost exactly the same amount over the expansion of the 1980s as do official poverty rates. This is perhaps not surprising since in-kind income did not grow in real terms over this time period.

2. The problem is *not* legislative changes in eligibility and benefits in public assistance programs. Some have suggested that the cuts Ronald Reagan implemented in the early 1980s offset the effects of economic growth. While it is true that welfare payments declined in real terms for poor families throughout the 1980s, this had little effect on poverty, largely because public assistance does little to actually move families above the poverty line. Most public assistance payments move recipients *closer* to the official poverty line, but the benefits are low enough that few families actually escape poverty because of public benefit payments. (The elderly, to whom we provide much more generous benefits, are an exception to this. Government assistance moves a substantial number of elderly persons and couples out of poverty. But the elderly were largely unaffected by the cuts of the early 1980s.)

3. The problem is *not* the changing demographic composition of the poor. Between the 1960s and the 1980s, the composition of the poor changed substantially. The share of the elderly declined, as did the share of poor married-couple families. An increasing share of the poor were single-parent families, typically single mothers. As it turns out, however, single-mother families are at least as responsive (or nonresponsive) to economic growth as other groups. If the composition of the poor had remained constant from the early 1960s through the 1980s, the poverty rate would have been just as unresponsive to the macro economy of the 1980s.

So what did happen? Let's start by discussing *why* economic growth would be expected to decrease poverty in the first place. Earnings, the most important component in most families' income, are the result of labor market effort multiplied by wages. How are these affected by the economic cycle?

The primary effect of economic growth on the distribution of income occurs through the availability of jobs. When the economy expands, employment grows and the demand for workers increases. Those who are unemployed, employed part-time, or not working at all, are most likely to benefit from employment expansions. And unemployed, part-time, and discouraged workers are disproportionately likely to be less-skilled individuals in low-income families. Those who are working 40 to 50 hours a week are typically unable to benefit as much from employment growth. In March 1993, when overall unemployment was 7 percent, unemployment among high school dropouts was 15 percent, among high school graduates it was 8 percent, while among college graduates it was just over 3 percent.[5] These unemployment differentials across skill levels have been relatively constant for many years in the U.S. economy.

Thus, when the economy expands, the main reason why those in families at the bottom of the income distribution catch up, relative to those in the middle, is that they gain more from the employment expansion that accompanies an economic boom. This clearly happened in the 1960s, when both the probability of working and weeks of work among the employed expanded more rapidly among persons in low-income families than in higher-income families. But it also happened in the 1980s. The evidence indicates that adults in low-income households took advantage of growing employment opportunities in the 1980s even more than they did in the earlier decades. Work effort was *more* responsive to changes in the economy in the 1980s than in the 1960s. If we look only at the growth in work behavior, we would have expected poverty to fall *faster* in the 1980s.

If labor market effort expanded as much in the 1980s as the 1960s, the only remaining factor is wages. In the 1960s, real wages expanded throughout the income distribution. GDP growth of 1 percent in the 1960s was correlated with a $2.18 increase in real weekly wages among workers in low-wage families. This expansion in wages reinforced the growth in employment occurring at the same time, so that workers both expanded their hours of work and earned more every hour. The result was that poverty plummeted during that decade.

Among the poorest groups in the population in the 1980s, however, real wages actually *fell* with economic growth. Both high school dropouts and high school graduates have experienced a steady decline in their earnings starting in about 1979 that has continued through the past fifteen years. The result was that the poor worked more during the economic expansion of the 1980s, but earned less per hour over time. Unlike the 1960s, these two effects *offset* each other. While poverty did decline, the decline was much more modest than expected as falling real wages limited the economic gains that increased labor market involvement should have produced. Both my own research and the research of others suggests that the difference between the responsiveness of poverty and of the income distribution to economic growth between the 1960s and the more recent decade is entirely due to these wage changes.

What's Happening to Wages?

Table 1 shows wage changes among men and women at different skill levels over the past twenty-five years. In order to abstract away from questions of changes in work effort, the table shows weekly wages (inflation adjusted) among nonelderly men and women who worked full time year-round. The decade between 1969 and 1979 was a bad decade for all workers. A series of recessions combined with high inflation rates left virtually all workers with lower wages in 1979 than they had earned ten years earlier. Since 1979, however, there has been sharp divergence in the wage changes experienced by more- and less-skilled workers. Average weekly wages among men who are high school dropouts have fallen by 15.6 percent, while they have risen by 15.7 percent among men who hold college degrees. The distribution of earnings has also widened among women, although this is largely because of big increases in earnings among more educated women. Women without a high school degree have faced virtually stagnant weekly earnings since 1969, while women with college degrees have seen their earnings grow by 31 percent. A growing body of literature has documented these changed among many groups using a wide variety of data sources. There are two primary conclusions that emerge from this literature.[6]

Table 1. Average Weekly Earnings by Years of School and Sex Among Nonelderly Adults Who Work Full Time and Full Year

Education level	Men			Women		
	1969	1979	1992	1969	1979	1992
Less than a high school degree	$489	$474	$400	$279	$281	$284
Percent change		-3.1	-15.6		+0.7	+1.1
High school degree	601	565	536	340	335	379
Percent change		-6.0	-5.1		-1.5	+13.1
Post-high school training, no college degree	699	626	641	388	377	451
Percent change		-10.4	+2.4		-2.8	+19.6
College or higher degree	911	841	973	523	489	642
Percent change		-7.7	+15.7		-6.5	+31.3

SOURCE: Tabulations from the Current Population Surveys, March 1970, 1980, and 1993, based on the civilian population ages 18-65. Inflation adjustments are based on the GDP deflator.

First, these wage changes are spread throughout the economy. They are occurring among men and women in virtually all industries and occupations. Less-skilled men in both manufacturing and nonmanufacturing industries have experienced similar real wage declines. Although the trends are strongest among younger workers, they are occurring among older workers as well.

Second, as is visible in table 1, there appear to be substantial gender differences in these trends. While the least-skilled women have not experienced wage increases, neither have they experienced the wage decline of their less-skilled brothers. While this has helped close the female-to-male wage gap, presumably those who wanted to bring men's and women's wages closer together did not want to do it by decreasing men's wages. It is also worth noting that wages among less-skilled women remain far below those of men. The average male high school dropout earned $400/week if he worked full time year-round in

1993, while the average female high school dropout earned only $284/week at full-time work.

What has caused these wage changes? That question is much discussed among economists, and a growing literature is attempting to explain various causal forces. In general, most analysts agree that it is changes in the demand for more- versus less-skilled labor that is driving these trends. In other words, employer demand for less-skilled labor has been falling over the last fifteen years, and this is driving down wages among this group. Two particular economy-wide changes have been strongly linked to these wage changes: the growing importance of international competition to U.S. firms and changing technology. Let's look at each of these in turn.

The Growing Internationalization of the U.S. Economy

As the U.S. economy is increasingly linked with the world economy, U.S. workers are in competition with workers around the globe. In this global labor market, skilled workers in the United States have a comparative advantage. The United States has more skilled, college-educated workers than any other country in the world. Less-skilled U.S. workers, however, are presumably at a comparative disadvantage relative to less-skilled workers in industrializing countries, such as those in the Pacific rim countries. Because the cost of living and the wage levels of less-skilled workers are substantially higher in the United States than elsewhere, demand for U.S. less-skilled labor might be expected to decrease while demand for less-skilled labor in lower-wage countries would rise.[7]

The evidence indicates that growth in international economic competition is not adequate by itself to fully explain U.S. wage changes. Those industries that have been experiencing rapid growth in international competition have not necessarily experienced greater declines in wages among less-skilled workers. But there is evidence that this trend is at least one of the causal reasons behind these shifts.

Changing Technology in the U.S. Economy

The other story for which there is substantial evidence is the possibility of technology shifts that have been demand-increasing for more skilled workers and demand-decreasing for less-skilled workers.[8] The rapid spread of computer-based technology in all industries and occupations is often mentioned as an example. In manufacturing industries, "smart" machines mean that these companies hire more computer programmers and computer-literate production line overseers and fewer workers to perform repetitive labor. In the service industries, the rapid spread of personal computers has decreased clerical demand and replaced many persons in less-skilled filing and data entry positions.

There is evidence to support both of these explanations for the wage changes of the past fifteen years, and almost surely both of them are happening at once. These changes are also linked to a variety of other institutional changes that are correlated with declining wages among the less skilled. For instance, union jobs continue to disappear in the United States, in part because of the economic pressures of changing trade and technology. Since unions typically raise the wages of the least skilled, this accounts for about one-fifth of the decline in wages among less-skilled workers.[9]

The most discouraging aspect of these two explanations is that neither of them promise any reversal of these wage trends. If anything, virtually all economists who have looked at these issues predict that the current trends toward a more internationalized economy and increasing use of "smart" technology, will continue in the near future. This means further declines in the earning ability of less-skilled workers.

Policy Implications

There are two major policy implications that emerge from the above discussion, both of them posing serious challenges to those who want to run effective policies to combat poverty in the United States.

Implication 1: Economic growth is unlikely to be an effective antipoverty tool in the near future.

For the past fifteen years, the employment expansions that occur when the economy grows have been offset by declines in real wages among less-skilled workers. As a result, the antipoverty "kick" that economic growth provided in earlier decades has not been available. To the extent that these wage trends are likely to continue, it is unreasonable to expect economic expansions during the 1990s to have substantial antipoverty effects.

Economic growth has historically been the most attractive antipoverty tool available. It provided broad-based income redistribution to low-income families at a time when the overall economic pie is growing. Thus, it required few hard political choices. In particular, it did not require higher taxes on middle- and upper-income families in order to provide services to lower-income families. There were also no administrative or overhead costs associated with a decline in poverty spurred by economic growth, since no government-run programs were required.

If economic growth is no longer available, this leaves us with two markedly less politically attractive alternatives. The first alternative is to pursue broad-based income redistribution through national cash-transfer programs for low-income families. This was originally proposed by Richard Nixon, who wanted to replace many small antipoverty programs with a nationally based (albeit relatively low) cash guarantee for the poorest families. While his plan was enacted for elderly families and resulted in the Supplemental Security Income program which provides substantial cash redistribution to elderly and disabled persons, it was politically unpalatable for other poor families. If anything, since Nixon's time, cash income redistribution has become even less politically viable in the United States. In the current environment, the push has been to decrease cash transfers to the nonelderly even further.

The second alternative is to give up on broad-based redistributional programs and instead work to design targeted programs that provide specific services to clearly defined groups of persons. This would include such programs as Headstart, food stamps, housing assistance, or employment and training efforts. These programs often link specific behavioral requirements to benefits. For instance, parents as well as children are required to actively participate in Headstart activities, while employment and training programs typically impose attendance or effort requirements on participants.

The welfare reform conversations over the last decade have been focused on how to effectively implement this second alternative. Extensive discussion at the federal and state level has focused on such issues as which groups to target, which behavioral requirements to impose, and how to efficiently provide these services to the targeted recipients.

In contrast to economic growth, such antipoverty efforts require extensive governmental planning and management. An organizational structure must be established to run programs and verify eligibility. In addition, such services clearly cost money up front. The administrative costs of implementing and managing these programs are often substantial and usually cost more than broad-based cash redistribution efforts.

Much of the frustration with our antipoverty system has been a frustration with such targeted, heavily managed services. Major discussion is occurring about how to streamline these programs to make them more efficient and to ensure that they treat more participants more effectively. Such discussion was perhaps inevitable in a world where targeted service-provision programs provide the major effort against poverty. Clearly, the ineffectiveness of overall economic growth as an antipoverty tool has left us with much less politically palatable alternatives.

Implication 2: Jobs alone will not solve poverty.

The other implication of the recent labor market changes is that employment is a less-effective way to escape poverty. Compared to thirty years ago, moving people out of poverty by moving them into employment is much harder. This is true for two reasons.

First, the changes in wages among less-skilled workers means that jobs pay less. Full-time work at the minimum wage provides only $8500, while the poverty line for a family of three is $12,500. Thus, efforts to move low-income adults out of poverty via employment will require more than just finding a job. Increases in employment will increase earnings, but for many low-income workers, this will not move them above the poverty line. Hence, in addition to programs designed to move people into jobs, we also have programs that supplement earnings by collecting child support from absent fathers, by subsidizing child care, or by supplementing wages through the Earned Income Tax Credit. Clearly, this costs more.

Second, as a growing share of the poor are single parents, this also limits the effectiveness of employment-based strategies, even in the absence of wage deterioration. Single parents often face more time constraints. They must act as the sole parent for their children as well as the primary family earner, making it harder for them to locate and keep a full-time job. In addition, many single parents must earn enough not just to cover their living expenses, but also to cover child care expenses. This increases the level of wages they need to make employment an effective strategy for escaping poverty.[10]

The United States has long focused on economic self-sufficiency as the preferred way out of poverty, at least among families headed by nonelderly adults. Our reluctance to provide cash assistance mirrors our insistence that the best way to help the poor is to assist them into employment in the mainstream economy. Unfortunately, when the jobs available to less-skilled adults pay less and less over time, the "employment strategy" becomes a harder one to implement as a way to assist families out of poverty.

The decline in real wages among less-skilled workers over the past fifteen years has seriously limited our ability to address poverty through government action. On the one hand, these changes have meant that we can no longer rely on economic expansions to do some of our work for us, decreasing poverty without explicit policies or programs on the part of the government. On the other hand, these changes have made it harder for us to operate targeted programs aimed at increasing employment and earnings among the poor. Given this, it is perhaps not surprising that there is a sense of frustration about U.S. antipoverty efforts. Let's be clear where the source of the problem lies, however. What have changed most significantly in the last fifteen years have been the economy and the labor market for poor workers. This makes the task harder for all who would design public programs to combat poverty. Not impossible, but harder.

NOTES

1. The poverty rate is the share of persons in the population who live in households whose cash income falls below the official U.S. poverty line. Poverty lines vary with household size.

2. Figure 1 puts GDP in 1993 dollars, which is to say that it is inflation-adjusted and expressed in terms of 1993 purchasing power.

3. These estimates are report in Blank (1993).

4. The following discussion is based on the evidence in Blank (1993) and Blank and Card (1993). Supporting evidence is also presented in Cutler and Katz (1991).

5. Data tabulated from the Current Population Survey tape, March 1993.

6. For a fuller discussion of these wage trends, see Levy and Murnane (1992), Danziger and Gottschalk (1993), or Juhn et al. (1993). For a discussion of the broader set of labor market changes that have affected less-skilled workers, see Blank (1995).

7. For evidence on the impact of trade competition on wage differentials, see Katz and Murphy (1992), Murphy and Welch (1993), and Sachs and Shatz (1994).

8. For evidence on the impact of changing technology on wages, see Bound and Johnson (1992), Davis and Haltiwanger (1991), or Berman, Bound, and Griliches (1993).

9. See Freeman (1993) or Card (1992).

10. For a further discussion of the implications of these changes on employment-based strategies, see Blank (1994).

References

Berman, Eli, John Bound, and Zvi Griliches. 1993. "Changes in the Demand for Skilled Labor within U.S. Manufacturing Industries: Evidence from the Annual Survey of Manufacturing." National Bureau of Economic Research, Working Paper No. 4255, January.

Blank, Rebecca M. 1993. "Why Were Poverty Rates So High in the 1980s?" In *Poverty and Prosperity in the USA in the Late Twentieth Century,* Dimitri Papadimitriou and Edward Wolff, eds. London: Macmillian.

_____. 1994. "The Employment Strategy: Public Policies to Increase Work and Earnings," In *Confronting Poverty: Prescriptions for Change,* Sheldon Danziger, Gary Sandefur and Daniel Weinberg, eds. Cambridge, MA: Harvard University Press.

_____. 1995. "Outlook for the U.S. Labor Market and Prospects for Low-Wage Entry Jobs." In *Welfare Reform and the Realities of the Job Market,* Demetra Nightingale and Robert Haveman, eds. Washington DC: Urban Institute Press.

Blank, Rebecca M., and Alan S. Blinder. 1986. "Macroeconomics, Income Distribution, and Poverty." In *Fighting Poverty,* Sheldon Danziger and Daniel Weinberg, eds. Cambridge, MA: Harvard University Press.

Blank, Rebecca M., and David Card. 1993. "Poverty, Income Distribution, and Growth: Are They Still Connected?" *Brookings Papers on Economic Activity* 2: 285-339.

Bound, John, and George Johnson. 1992. "Changes in the Structure of Wages in the 1980s: An Evaluation of Alternative Explanations," *American Economic Review* 82, 3 (June): 371-392.

Card, David. 1992. "The Effect of Unions on the Distribution of Wages: Redistribution or Relabelling?" National Bureau of Economic Research Working Paper No. 4195, October.

Cutler, David M., and Lawrence F. Katz. 1991. "Macroeconomic Performance and the Disadvantaged," *Brooking Papers on Economic Activity* 2: 1-61.

Danziger, Sheldon, and Peter Gottschalk. 1993. *Uneven Tides: Rising Inequality in America.* New York: Russell Sage Foundation.

Davis, Steve J., and John Haltiwanger. 1991. "Wage Dispersion Between and Within U.S. Manufacturing Plants: 1963-86," *Brookings Papers on Economic Activity: Microeconomics* 1: 115-180.

Freeman, Richard B. 1993. "How Much Has De-Unionization Contributed to the Rise in Male Earnings Inequality?" In *Uneven Tides: Rising Inequality in America.* Sheldon Danziger and Peter Gottschalk, eds. New York: Russell Sage Foundation.

Juhn, Chinhui, Kevin M. Murphy, and Brooks Pierce. 1993. "Wage Inequality and the Rise in Returns to Skill," *Journal of Political Economy* 101, 3: 410-442.

Katz, Lawrence F., and Kevin M. Murphy. 1992. "Changes in Relative Wages, 1963-87: Supply and Demand Factors," *Quarterly Journal of Economics* 107, 1: 35-78.

Levy, Frank, and Richard J. Murnane. 1993. "U.S. Earnings Levels and Earnings Inequality: A Review of Recent Trends and Proposed Explanation," *Journal of Economic Literature* 30, 3: 1333-1381.

Murphy, Kevin M., and Finis Welch. 1993. "Industrial Change and the Rising Importance of Skill." In *Uneven Tides: Rising Inequality in America,* Sheldon Danziger and Peter Gottschalk, eds. New York: Russell Sage Foundation.

Sachs, Jeffrey D., and H. J. Shatz. 1994. "Trade and Jobs in U.S. Manufacturing," *Brookings Papers on Economic Activity* 1: 1-69.

Regional Poverty and Inequality in the United States

John P. Formby
University of Alabama

Poverty and income inequality are related, but distinct, aspects of the size distribution of income within a society. At the outset, it is important to understand the difference and relationship between these concepts. Poverty and inequality can be explained and illustrated by using a simple ordered income distribution. Before doing this, however, it is helpful to provide some basic intuition concerning poverty and inequality that corresponds to widely held views of disparities in income and wealth. The conversation supposedly took place between F. Scott Fitzgerald and Ernest Hemingway concerning the differences in the behavior of ordinary Americans and the wealthy. Fitzgerald is reported to have said, "You know Ernest, rich people are different from us." Hemingway replied, "You're right, rich people have more money than we do." From the perspective of the economist, Hemingway was correct. It is income and wealth that matter, and they are at the essence of both poverty and inequality. The fact that some people have larger shares of the income and wealth of a society and others have smaller shares gives rise to the basic notion of economic inequality. The individuals and families with the smallest shares may be, but are not necessarily, poor. Poverty arises when the levels of income and wealth are so low that the individuals are unable to acquire the market basket of goods that are deemed essential for a minimally decent standard of living.

Some Basic Concepts of Poverty and Inequality

The basic ideas underlying poverty and inequality, which are advanced in a very informal manner above, suggest that income inequality is a *relative income* concept, whereas poverty is an *absolute income* concept. While these are not the only approaches to defining and measuring poverty and inequality, they are the most widely used, especially in the United States. In fact, an absolute income definition is officially incorporated into the statutory definition of poverty in the United States, whereas relative income inequality is the dominant perspective adopted by both policy makers and academic researchers around the world. The difference between relative income and absolute income and between inequality and poverty can be made clear with a simple income distribution. An income distribution is merely a list of incomes, or more formally a vector of incomes, of a group of individuals, families, or households. To illustrate the key concepts, two population groups that reside in region N and S are considered. To keep things simple, it is assumed that there are only five individuals in each region. The incomes are ordered from lowest to highest and shown in column 2 of tables 1a and 1b. The information in columns 1 and 2 shows the ordered absolute income distributions, which are plotted and shown in figure 1a. Now suppose that in both regions an income of $16 is required to purchase the market basket of goods that are deemed to be essential for a decent, but minimum, standard of living. The income of $16 is the *poverty threshold* and is represented by the poverty line in figure 1a. Given a poverty line of $16, one individual, A, in region N has an absolute income below the poverty threshold and is therefore classified as poor, while two persons, F and G, in region S are below the poverty line.

The relative incomes of individual persons residing in region N and region S are given by their respective proportionate shares of total regional income and are shown in column 4 of tables 1a and 1b. The relative shares (proportions) of persons and incomes are cumulated in columns 5 and 6. The cumulative shares of persons and incomes can be used to construct Lorenz curves, which provide the most basic way of representing economic inequality in a society or region. The relative income distributions in regions N and S are depicted by the Lorenz curves shown in figure 1b, which are obtained by plotting the cumulative shares of persons and incomes in columns 5 and 6. Relative inequality in a region is shown by the deviations of the Lorenz curves away from the 45$°$ degree line in figure 1b, which represents complete equality in the distribution of income.

Table 1. Two Simple Income Distributions—Regions N and S

1a. Region N

		Shares (proportions)		Cumulative shares	
Person (1)	Incomes $^{a} (2)	Persons (3)		Income (4)	Persons (5)
A	12	.20	.0923	.20	.0923
B	18	.20	.1385	.40	.2308
C	22	.20	.1692	.60	.4000
D	28	.20	.2154	.80	.6154
E	50	.20	.3846	1.00	1.0000
	$130	1.00	1.00		

1b. Region S

		Shares (proportions)		Cumulative shares	
Person (1)	Incomes $^{a} (2)	Persons (3)		Income (4)	Persons (5)
F	10	.20	.10	.20	.10
G	15	.20	.15	.40	.25
H	20	.20	.20	.60	.45
I	25	.20	.25	.80	.70
J	30	.20	.30	1.00	1.00
	$100	1.00	1.00		

a. Incomes are ordered from lowest to highest.

Figure 1b tells the entire story about income inequality in regions N and S, but it deserves emphasis that the relative income distributions tell us nothing about regional poverty. The Lorenz curves in figure 1b are consistent with the existence of extreme poverty or with the total absence of poverty in regions N and S. Similarly, figure 1a conveys much about poverty in regions N and S, but little about income inequality. In summary, if we wish to know about economic inequality, we must focus on relative incomes, and the most basic method for doing this is to look directly at the Lorenz curves, which show the distribution of relative incomes. If the goal is to learn about poverty, the task is

Figure 1a. Absolute Incomes and the Poverty Line in Two Regions

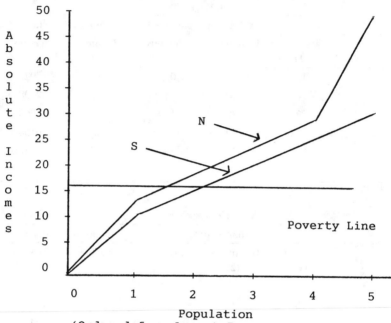

Population
(Ordered from Lowest Income to Highest)

somewhat more complex. However, the basic starting point is with the absolute income distributions and the poverty line, which are depicted in figure 1a.

Widely Used Measures of Poverty and Inequality

Poverty and inequality can be measured in a variety of different ways, but all build upon the absolute and relative income concepts described above. It is useful to briefly identify and describe several of the most widely used measures that will be utilized in reporting on regional poverty and inequality below. The United States is one of the few countries that has an official definition of poverty, widely referred to as the *headcount ratio* measure of poverty or, more simply, the pov-

Figure 1b. Lorenz Curves for Two Regions

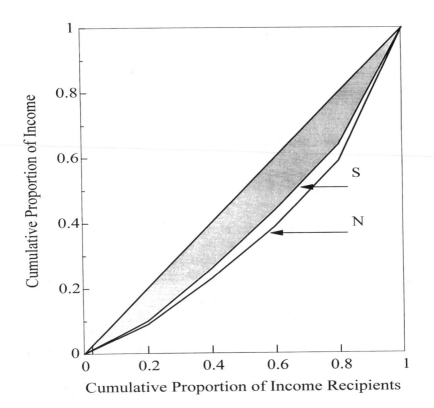

erty rate. You begin with the poverty line and count the number of persons with incomes below the poverty threshold; the headcount ratio (poverty rate) is simply the proportion of the population with incomes below the poverty line. For example, in our simple income distributions, for a $16 poverty line, the headcount ratio measure of poverty in region N is .2, which means one out of five persons is poor. In region S, the poverty rate is .4, which means that 40 percent of the population (two out of five) is poor.

Several difficulties with the headcount measure of poverty will be discussed below, but for now it is sufficient to note that it is an intuitively appealing and easily understood concept that captures an important dimension of poverty. However, for the reasons explained in the next section, the official headcount measure of poverty fails to incorporate all relevant aspects of poverty, and it is essential that it be supplemented with better measures of income and additional dimensions of poverty that encapsulate the missing information.

It is apparent from figure 1a that the extent of poverty in a region depends upon where the poverty line is drawn. If the line is drawn at $8 rather than $16, there are no poor people in either region! Alternatively, if the poverty line is $23, the poverty rate stands at .6 in both regions. Thus, two important issues in poverty measurement are: how should the poverty line be determined, and exactly where should it be drawn? This issue is returned to below, but as a starting point it is helpful to explain how the official U.S. poverty line was originally determined, and how it is redrawn each year. The poverty threshold levels of income were developed in the early 1960s by Mollie Orshansky and her colleagues in the Social Security Administration. Using detailed consumption expenditure data from the 1950s, it was estimated that, on average, U.S. families spent approximately one-third of their cash income on food. Orshansky (1965) used these food expenditures to estimate what it would cost in 1964 to purchase the U.S. Department of Agriculture's Economy Food Market Basket, which contained the requisite nutrients for "temporary or emergency use when funds are low." These costs were then multiplied by three to obtain the poverty threshold level of income. The expenditure studies revealed that spending on food varied with the size of the family and with the age of the family head. Families with an elderly head were determined to spend significantly less on food than other families, and larger families were found to spend more than smaller families. As a consequence, the poverty threshold incomes were different depending upon the size of the family and whether the head was aged 65 or older. In 1969 the Orshansky income thresholds were officially adopted by the federal government for purposes of measuring poverty. To change the official poverty line across time, the Orshansky thresholds are deflated by using the consumer price index. Table 2 shows the poverty thresholds for 1992 for different sized families and for nonelderly heads.

Like poverty, income inequality can be measured in a variety of ways. A method that yields unanimous agreement concerning inequality comparisons is referred to as Lorenz dominance (Atkinson 1970). In figure 1b the Lorenz curve of region S is closer to the line of com-

Table 2. U.S. Poverty Thresholds in 1992 by Family Size, Number of Children and Age of Household Head

Family size	Poverty Thresholds ($) by Number of Children							
	None	One	Two	Three	Four	Five	Six	Seven	Eight+
One person									
Under 65	7,299								
65 or over	6,729								
Two Persons									
HH under 65	9,395	9,670							
HH 65 or over	8,480	9,634							
Three persons	10,974	11,293	11,304						
Four persons	14,471	14,708	14,228	14,277					
Five persons	17,451	17,705	17,163	16,743	16,487				
Six persons	20,072	20,152	19,737	19,339	18,747	18,396			
Seven persons	23,096	23,240	22,743	21,751	20,998	20,171			
Eight persons	25,831	26,059	25,590	25,179	24,596	23,855	23,085	22,889	
Nine+ persons	31,073	31,223	30,808	30,459	29,887	29,099	28,387	28,211	27,124

SOURCE: U.S. Bureau of the Census (1993).
NOTE: HH denotes household head.

plete equality than the Lorenz curve of region N. S is said to Lorenz dominate N, which means that regardless of the specific numerical measure (index) used, inequality will always be less in S than in N. A corollary to Atkinson's Lorenz dominance theorem is that if the Lorenz curves of interest intersect, two summary indices of inequality can always be found that yield a conflicting ranking of inequality; one index will rank region S as more equal, whereas the second index will rank region N as more equal. In our example, Lorenz dominance prevails, and there is no need to worry about the problem of conflicting index numbers. Therefore, any number of inequality indices can be chosen to represent the level of inequality.

The Gini index is the most widely used and discussed measure of inequality, and its intuitive meaning can be easily conveyed using the Lorenz curves in figure 1b. The Gini index varies between 0 and 1.0, with zero indicating complete equality and 1.0 representing the most extreme inequality imaginable (complete inequality). The Gini index is larger the more the Lorenz curve bows away from the $45°$ line, which represents a perfectly equal income distribution. Thus, one can look at figure 1b and see immediately that region N has a larger Gini index than region S because at every point its Lorenz curve is further away from the line of equality. The Gini index has a simple geometric interpretation that is related to the line of equality; the Gini is always equal to twice the area between the $45°$ line (perfect equality) in figure 1b and the Lorenz curve of interest. In our example involving regions S and N, taking the necessary integrals and doing the calculations reveals that $G_N = 0.276$ and $G_S = 0.207$. Thus, according to the Gini measure of inequality, income inequality is *one-third* greater in region N than region S. Like the headcount poverty measure, the Gini index is not a perfect measure. For this reason the Lorenz dominance is the primary method relied upon in discussing income inequality below. However, because it is easy to interpret and widely used, Gini indices of inequality are also presented. The Gini index is also used when we incorporate the distribution of income among the poor into an expanded and improved measure of poverty.

Headcount Measures of Poverty and Dominance Measures of Inequality

This section reviews the broad picture of regional poverty and inequality that emerges when one considers the official U.S. poverty statistics and naively applies the Lorenz dominance technique to gauge regional differences in income inequality. The historical relation between the absolute and relative income in the South compared to the rest of the United States is also briefly discussed. Measurement issues and more complex empirical estimates are considered in the sections that follow.

Official Poverty Statistics and Comparable Estimates for 1939 and 1949

Official poverty statistics are available for each year beginning in 1959, and Smolensky, Danziger and Gottschalk (1988) have extended the series backward by providing comparable estimates for 1939 and 1949.[1] The pattern of overall headcount measures of poverty is shown in figure 2. Poverty in America fell dramatically in the 1940s, 1950s, and 1960s, reaching an historical low point in 1973. Beginning in the mid-1970s, the trend in headcount poverty has been mildly upward, with cyclical swings and peaks occurring shortly after the trough of recessions. The double dip recessions in the early 1980s were particularly severe, and the headcount poverty rate reached 15.2 percent in 1983, the highest level in the last quarter century.

In 1992 the official poverty rate was 14.5 percent, which was approximately the same level as in 1966, when the War on Poverty was at its most intense level. However, the U.S. population in 1992 was 255 million, compared to 196 million in 1966. Therefore, while the headcount poverty rate is approximately the same in these two years, there were 8.5 million more Americans living in poverty in 1992 than 1966.

Figure 2. Headcount Poverty Rates Using the Official U.S. Poverty Line and Measurement Procedures, 1939-1992

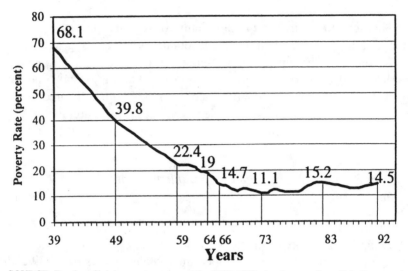

SOURCE: For the official poverty measures for 1959-1992, the data are from U.S. Bureau of the Census (1993). The estimates for 1939 and 1949 are from Smolensky, Danziger, and Gottschalk (1988).

Table 3 shows the headcount poverty rates among major U.S. regions for selected years beginning with 1959, which is the earliest date for which official poverty statistics are available. Three implications are suggested by table 3. First, when viewed in terms of the official headcount measures, the South regularly has more poverty than other regions. This is most apparent in 1959, but continues to be true even in the most recent data. The South's poverty rate was twice the level of the rest of the country in 1959, and approximately one-half of all persons living in poverty resided in a region that accounted for only 30 percent of the U.S. population. Second, the official statistics suggest that poverty is generally lower in the Northeast than other regions. Finally, in each region and the United States as a whole, the incidence of poverty among children is approximately 150 percent of the overall poverty rate for comparable population.[2]

Table 3. Regional Poverty Rates Using the Official Poverty Line and Measurement Procedures, 1959-1992

	Northeast	Midwest	West	South	U.S.
1992	12.3 (19.7)	12.9 (19.4)	14.3 (21.3)	16.3 (24.6)	14.5 (21.7)
1989	10.0	11.9	12.5	15.4	12.8
1979	10.4	9.7	10.0	15.0	11.7
1969	8.6	9.6	10.4	17.9	12.1
1959	16.0[a]			35.4	22.4

SOURCE: The official poverty statistics for 1992 are from U.S. Bureau of the Census (1993). For 1959-1979 the statistics are from U.S. Bureau of the Census (1981). The data for 1989 are from U.S. Bureau of the Census (1990).
NOTE: Figures in parenthesis denote the poverty rates for children in major regions.
a. Applies to the non-South, i.e., the Northeast, Midwest, and West combined.

Income Inequality

Unlike poverty statistics, there are neither official U.S. government income distribution statistics nor official measures of economic inequality. However, there are a number of periodic surveys of large samples of American households that provide information that can be used to measure income inequality. A large sample is required to reliably gauge regional income inequality, and the two sources most often used in the U.S. are the Annual Demographic File of the Current Population Survey (March CPS survey) and the economic surveys conducted as a part of the decennial Census of Population.[3] We use both sources of information in our measures of regional and overall U.S. inequality. Income distribution statistics that are consistent across time are available beginning in the late 1940s. Figures 3a and 3b show Lorenz curves from the decennial Census of Population for the family income distribution in 1949, 1979, and 1989. Figure 3a shows that the 1979 Lorenz curve dominates the 1949 curve, which means that income inequality declined over this extended period. Figure 3b depicts the much discussed rise in U.S. income inequality in the 1980s and shows that 1979 Lorenz dominates 1989.[4]

Figure 3a. Lorenz Curves for the United States, 1949 and 1979

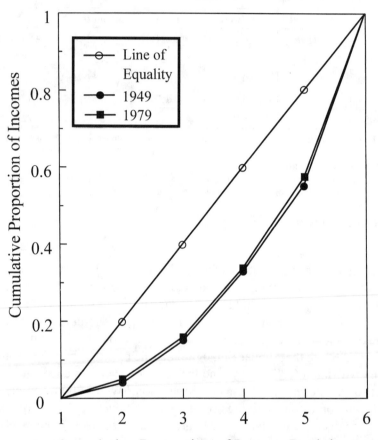

The substantial rise in income inequality in the nation as a whole in the 1980s was accompanied by increases in inequality in each of the major regions. The pattern of regional inequality suggested by the family income distributions drawn from the decennial Census of Population in 1989 is shown in table 4 and figure 4. Pairwise comparisons of the Lorenz ordinates in table 4 reveal that in 1989 the Midwest Lorenz curve dominates each of the other major regions, while the South is

Figure 3b. Lorenz Curves for the United States, 1979 and 1989

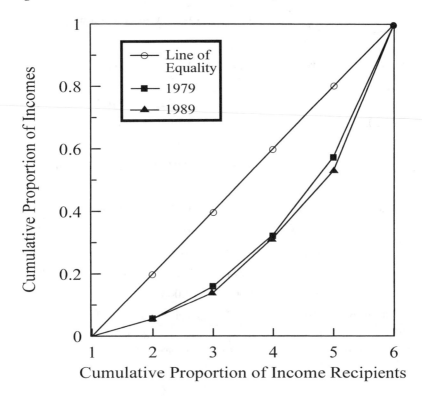

Lorenz-dominated by all regions. Note that in columns 2 and 5 of table 4 the Gini coefficient for the Northeast is slightly smaller than in the West, which suggests more equality. However, inspection of the Lorenz ordinates reveals that the Lorenz curves in these two regions intersect. Under these conditions it is always possible to find at least two inequality indices that yield contradictory ranking of regional inequality. This needs to be recognized in interpreting the Gini coefficients for the Northeast and West. Figure 4 shows Hesse diagrams of the inequality orderings of the regions in 1989. The Lorenz ranking of the Northeast and West appear on the same level, which means that they cannot be ranked using the Lorenz dominance criterion.

Table 4. Regional and Overall U.S. Income Inequality in 1980

Cumulative Proportion of Families (1)	Cumulative Proportion of Incomes				
	Northeast (2)	Midwest (3)	South (4)	West (5)	U.S. (6)
.10	0.013	0.014	0.012	0.014	0.013
.20	0.044	0.048	0.041	0.045	0.044
.30	0.091	0.096	0.085	0.009	0.089
.40	0.151	0.157	0.042	0.149	0.147
.50	0.224	0.233	0.263	0.221	0.22
.60	0.312	0.324	0.301	0.309	0.309
.70	0.413	0.429	0.406	0.411	0.412
.80	0.539	0.552	0.53	0.538	0.535
.90	0.704	0.714	0.695	0.703	0.702
1.00	1.000	1.000	1.000	1.000	1.000
Gini Index	0.407	0.392	0.421	0.410	0.411

SOURCE: Calculated from summary income distribution data from the 1990 U.S. Census Population. Estimates are made using a cubic spline procedure. Pareto's Law is used to estimate the mean
of the open-ended income class.

The South's Income Distribution in Historical Perspective

The official poverty statistics and the income distribution statistics
from the last five Census of Populations indicate two important pieces
of information concerning regional income distributions. The South
appears to have lower absolute incomes at the bottom of the income
distribution, hence greater headcount poverty and more relative income
inequality than the rest of the country. These results are consistent with
indirect historical evidence presented by Williamson (1977), which
strongly suggests that the South had a lower average family income
and greater income inequality throughout the period 1820 to 1930.
Thus, the patterns that are observed in reviewing official poverty statistics and Census income distribution data seem to represent a continuation of the historical pattern of the 19th century. However, Wright

Figure 4. Lorenz and Gini Rankings of Regional Family Income Distributions*

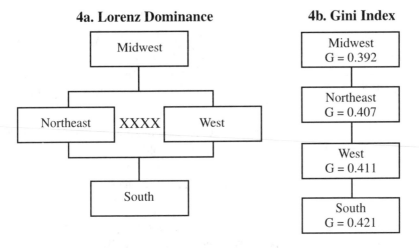

4a. Lorenz Dominance

4b. Gini Index

*Estimated from summary income distribution statistics using a cubic spline procedure.

(1987) has emphasized that fundamental changes in the 1940s, 1950s, and 1960s resulted in the emergence of a national labor market, which diminished regional differences in the American labor force. This in turn has immense implications for regional income distributions. These changes are discussed further below.

Measurement Issues in Evaluating Regional Poverty and Income Inequality

There are a number of difficulties in the measurement of income distributions that affect the reliability of poverty and inequality measures. Only the major issues most relevant to evaluating regional poverty and inequality in the United States are discussed. In brief, the chief problems associated with measuring poverty are as follows:

1. The official poverty statistics are based upon "Census money income," which excludes noncash transfers such as food stamps and the subsidized component in public housing as well as taxes.[5]

2. The official poverty line is essentially arbitrary and could be drawn at higher or lower income thresholds. In practice, the only change in the official poverty line across time involves inflating the Orshansky income thresholds to correct for changes in the Consumer Price Index.

3. The Orshansky food expenditure-based income thresholds involve a specific equivalent scale for households, and it is now widely recognized that there are a large number of such equivalent scales that could be used to construct alternative measures of poverty.

4. The official poverty line fails to take into account regional and urban-rural variations in the cost of living, which results in an overstatement of poverty in regions with low living costs and an understatement in high-cost regions.

5. Headcount poverty fails to measure the intensity or severity of poverty; a person whose income is far below the poverty line is treated as if he or she is equivalent to a person who is barely below poverty. Similarly, a person who is permanently poor (due, say, to a disability that results in zero or low earnings) is treated as equivalent to a person who is temporarily down and out, but who will soon recover and exit from the poverty group.

6. Given a particular poverty line, the official poverty statistics fail to consider the distribution of income among the low-income population.

7. The official poverty statistics are based upon the March CPS survey and are subject to well-known sampling error problems.

There are also measurement issues that are encountered in assessing income inequality. Fortunately, they are not nearly so severe as in the case of poverty. As noted above, there is no official government measure of inequality, nor is there anything comparable to a poverty line in inequality measurement. Moreover, inequality is a relative income concept, and there is generally no need to make adjustments for regional differences in the cost of living. Further, there is wide agreement that

Lorenz dominance is the most general method of gauging inequality, and the measurement procedures are straightforward. Nevertheless, there are a number of problems worth noting.

First, a fundamental measurement problem arises when Lorenz curves intersect. Under these conditions inequality indices can yield contradictory results. An approach that has evolved in the empirical study of inequality is to calculate a number of popular inequality indices to determine whether they in fact conflict.[6] This approach misses the point and is really not satisfactory; when Lorenz curves cross perfectly, defensible inequality indices can always be uncovered that yield conflicting rankings. Fortunately, there has been some recent progress on this issue and a better procedure based upon dominance principles is now available and can be applied when Lorenz curves intersect.[7]

A second problem in assessing inequality is identical to one encountered in evaluating poverty; income distribution statistics are invariably based upon surveys and are subject to sampling error. The wide availability of micro data that can be used in measuring inequality has led to the development of statistical inference procedures that take sampling errors into account. These procedures also allow researchers to test scientific hypotheses concerning both regional poverty and inequality. Thus, progress has been made on this measurement problem as well. However, the availability and wide use of micro data raises additional measurement questions that must be addressed if differences and changes in regional inequality are to be properly addressed. These include the following:

1. When micro data are used, the researcher can define the income-receiving unit in several different ways, and it is well known that the choice of the recipient unit can influence the resulting measures of relative inequality. Alternative definitions of the recipient include families, households, persons, spending units, and the equivalent number of adults in a household, family, or spending unit.

2. If the equivalent number of adults is used as the recipient unit, which of the many adult equivalence scales should be used? The choice of the scale may affect the outcome.

3. What accounting period should be used in measuring income ine-quality? Typically one year is used, but this is arbitrary. Most (but not all) micro data sets including the widely used March CPS sur-vey allow for longer periods, and some surveys allow for shorter periods. Typically, the researcher has a range of options concern-ing the time period over which income is measured, and the choice can influence measured inequality.[8]

Expanded Measures of Regional Poverty and Inequality

This section provides expanded and improved measures of regional poverty and income inequality that rely upon micro data and correct for some (but not all) of the measurement difficulties outlined above. We begin by discussing Amartya Sen's distribution-sensitive index of poverty and then report on recent research by Bishop, Formby and Zheng (1994) that presents new evidence on regional poverty based upon the Census money income used in making official poverty esti-mates and a more comprehensive income measure that includes the effects of direct taxes and noncash transfers. These expanded estimates correct for the problem of sampling error and consider the implications of alternative poverty lines. The section concludes with a discussion of expanded measures of regional income inequality that are provided by Bishop, Formby and Thistle (1992, 1994).

Sen Measures of Regional Poverty

Sen (1976) argues persuasively that poverty should be measured and evaluated using a three-prong approach that considers the headcount of a population living below the poverty line, the income shortfalls of the poor, and the inequality of incomes among the poor. According to Sen, neither headcount nor income gap measures of poverty, either taken together or used alone, are adequate measures of poverty. In Sen's view, an acceptable measure of poverty must be *distribution-sensitive,* which means that a transfer of income among the low-income popula-tion must be reflected in the overall measure of poverty index. In par-ticular, if income is redistributed from an extremely poor person to a higher income person below the poverty line, the measure of poverty should increase, not decrease. To better understand this point, again consider the simple income distribution in regions N and S, shown in table 1. If the poverty threshold is $22 then three persons in each region are classified as poor according to the headcount measure of poverty. Now suppose the government's Antipoverty Agency declares a War on Poverty and uses its powers to redistribute $3 from the poorest person in each region, A and F, to the least poor person, C and H. The transfers raise the incomes of C and H so that these individuals are moved above the poverty line. Thus, headcount poverty falls in both regions and the poverty fighting agency can claim success. However, the redistribution from an intensely poor person to a less poor person always increases relative inequality among the poor. One of Sen's great accomplishments demonstrates that when the headcount ratio and average income shortfall (poverty gap) of the poor are both constant, a rise in income inequality among the poor necessarily increases the economic deprivation among the poor. This is the case irrespective of whether the rise in income inequality among the poor is caused by market forces or a change in government policies.

To avoid these difficulties Sen proposes a poverty index that is simultaneously sensitive to headcount poverty, the income shortfall of the poor (poverty gap), and the distribution of income among the poor. His index is said to be a "distribution-sensitive measure of poverty" and is now widely referred to simply as the Sen index. To incorporate all relevant dimensions of poverty, Sen proposes an index that is equal to the aggregated income gaps between each poor person's income and the poverty line, weighted by each individual's relative rank among the poor. Sen shows that such an index, which is denoted as S, can be written as:

$$S - H\left[I + (1 - I)G_p\frac{q}{q + 1}\right]$$

where H is the headcount poverty ratio, I is the ratio of the average income shortfall-to-poverty line (hereinafter referred to as the poverty gap ratio), G_p is the Gini coefficient of income inequality among the poor, and q is the number of people below the poverty threshold.

Bishop, Formby and Zheng (1994) use the Sen index and its components—the headcount poverty ratio (H), the poverty gap ratio (I), and the Gini coefficient of income inequality among the poor (G_p)—to provide expanded measures of regional poverty in the United States in 1979, 1985, and 1990. They devise new statistical inference procedures, consider two distinct income measures, and report their results for three different poverty lines. They analyze the official poverty line and make use of Census money income, so one set of their estimates is directly comparable to the official poverty measures. They also consider poverty lines 25 percent above and 25 percent below the official (Orshansky) thresholds and present evidence for a comprehensive income measure as well as the more restrictive concept used in the official poverty statistics. The different income measures have considerable impact upon regional poverty, and it is helpful to briefly elaborate on how income is measured. The differences between Census money income and the comprehensive income concept measure that Bishop, Formby and Zheng (1994) use are revealed by the following definitions:

$$
\begin{array}{l}
\textit{Census} \\
\textit{Money} \\
\textit{Income}
\end{array}
=
\left[
\begin{array}{c}
\textit{Wages and Salaries} \\
+ \\
\textit{Self-Employment Income} \\
+ \\
\textit{Dividends, Rents and Interest} \\
+ \\
\textit{Cash Transfers (e.g., AFDC)}
\end{array}
\right]
$$

and

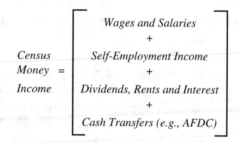

$$
\begin{array}{l}
\textit{Comprehensive} \\
\textit{Income}
\end{array}
=
\begin{array}{l}
\textit{Census} \\
\textit{Money} \\
\textit{Income}
\end{array}
+
\left[
\begin{array}{cc}
\textit{Market Value} & \textit{Federal Income} \\
\textit{of Food Stamps} & \textit{Taxes} \\
+ & + \\
\textit{Market Value} & \textit{State Income} \\
\textit{of Housing Subsidies} & \textit{Taxes} \\
+ & + \\
\textit{Market Value} & \textit{Payroll Taxes} \\
\textit{of Energy Subsidies} & - \\
+ & \\
\textit{Market Value} & \textit{Earned Income} \\
\textit{of SchoolLunch Program} & \textit{Tax Credit} \\
+ & \\
\textit{Market Value} & \\
\textit{of WIC Program} &
\end{array}
\right]
$$

Table 5 summarizes the regional Sen poverty indices for 1979, 1985, and 1990 that are estimated using the official poverty line. The changes in poverty across time that Bishop, Formby and Zheng (1994) find to be statistically significant from zero are indicated by asterisks. Tables 6 and 7 show comparable information when estimates are made using poverty lines that are respectively 25 percent below and 25 percent above the official poverty thresholds. Inspection of tables 5, 6, and 7 reveals that the major impact of moving the poverty line up or down is to increase or decrease measured poverty in each of the regions. In one instance (the West, comprehensive income, 1979-1985) changing the poverty line influences the finding concerning whether a rise in poverty is statistically significant. However, for the most part, drawing the poverty line at a higher or lower income threshold has little impact on the statistical findings concerning changes in regional poverty across time.

To address the question of which U.S. region has the least poverty and which region has the most we summarize Bishop, Formby and Zheng's statistical rankings of Sen indices using the Hesse diagrams in figure 5. Figures 5a, 5b, and 5c show the orderings of regional poverty in 1979, 1985, and 1990 in terms of the Census money income, while figures 5d, 5e and 5f show the regional orderings for the same years in terms of comprehensive income. In each Hesse diagram, regions with the lowest level of poverty are at the top of the diagram, regions that have Sen indices that are not significantly different are ranked on the same level, and regions ranked at the bottom have the most severe poverty. Figure 5 clearly illustrates the advantages of an inference-based analysis of poverty; five of the six Hesse diagrams show examples of regions that are not significantly different from one another, a finding that is virtually impossible using simple comparisons of point estimates.

Now consider the regional rankings in terms of Census money income shown in figures 5a, 5b, and 5c. The statistical rankings suggest two general conclusions. The Midwest and West are at the top diagram, indicating that they have significantly less poverty when evaluated in terms of Sen's distribution-sensitive measure. Conversely, the South and Northeast are almost always at the bottom, which means these regions have significantly more poverty than the West and Midwest when Census money is the metric. A quite different pattern emerges when the comprehensive income measure is used. The Mid-

Table 5. Sen Indices of Regional Poverty Estimated Using the Official Poverty Line, 1979, 1985, and 1990

5a. Census Money Income

Time period	Northeast	Midwest	South	West
1979	0.044	0.035	0.059	0.038
1985	0.081	0.061	0.073	0.056
1990	0.083	0.064	0.086	0.071
Percent change 1979-1985	85.2**	115.9**	25.5**	25.9**
Percent change 1985-1990	2.2	3.8	17.2**	25.9**

5b. Comprehensive Income

Time period	Northeast	Midwest	South	West
1979	0.022	0.020	0.025	0.027
1985	0.025	0.027	0.038	0.032
1990	0.069	0.048	0.067	0.061
Percent change 1970-1985	15.5	32.8**	48.6**	17.5**
Percent change 1985-1990	172.3**	80.1**	81.2**	88.2**

**Significant at the 1 percent level.

west continues to be ranked at the top; in each of the years considered, the Midwest's Sen index is lower or as low as any other region. However, in the other regions there are significant changes in Sen index rankings. This is most dramatic for the Northeast. In 1979 and 1985, poverty measured in terms of comprehensive income in the Northeast was no different from the Midwest and was significantly less than in the West and South. But in 1990, the Northeast's Sen index was significantly larger than those of the West and Midwest and had increased to a level such that it was not significantly different from the Sen index in the South.

Table 6. Sen Indices of Regional Poverty Estimated Using a Poverty Line 25 Percent Below the Official Threshold, 1979, 1985, and 1990

6a. Census Money Income

Time period	Northeast	Midwest	South	West
1979	0.024	0.020	0.034	0.024
1985	0.051	0.040	0.050	0.035
1990	0.054	0.041	0.057	0.043
Percent change 1979-1985	111.6**	100.0**	44.2**	48.1**
Percent change 1985-1990	5.9	2.5	14.5**	22.6**

6b. Comprehensive Income

Time period	Northeast	Midwest	South	West
1979	0.013	0.013	0.034	0.018
1985	0.015	0.017	0.050	0.020
1990	0.039	0.026	0.057	0.035
Percent change 1970-1985	14.4	30.7**	59.7**	8.2
Percent change 1985-1990	159.6**	56.6**	66.1**	116.8**

**Significant at the 1 percent level.

The entire pattern of Sen measures of regional poverty among regions and across time suggests the following conclusions. The Midwest is at the top of the rankings in all but one case (Census money income, 1985), where it is ranked in the second position. The South is generally ranked toward the bottom of the Hesse diagrams, indicating that it usually has significantly greater poverty than other regions for both measures of income. In contrast, the ranking of the Northeast and West are sensitive to the income definition and the time period. For example, in 1979, the West is ranked at the top of the Census income diagram (lowest poverty) but at the bottom of the comprehensive

**Table 7. Sen Indices of Regional Poverty Estimated Using a Poverty Line
25 Percent Above the Official Threshold, 1979, 1985, and 1990**

7a. Census Money Income

Time period	Northeast	Midwest	South	West
1979	0.067	0.054	0.086	0.055
1985	0.114	0.084	0.100	0.080
1990	0.112	0.087	0.118	0.101
Percent change 1979-1985	70.0**	56.4**	16.3**	47.0**
Percent change 1985-1990	-1.7	3.9	17.9**	26.1*

7b. Comprehensive Income

Time period	Northeast	Midwest	South	West
1979	0.034	0.031	0.040.	0.040
1985	0.040	0.041	0.055	0.048
1990	0.101	0.074	0.1002	0.092
Percent change 1970-1985	16.3	32.0**	36.8**	20.8
Percent change 1985-1990	153.3**	80.1**	83.5**	90.9**

*Significant at the 5 percent level.
**Significant at the 1 percent level.

income diagram (highest poverty). The most striking differences, which
reflect fundamental changes, occurred in the Northeast. For example, in
1985 the Northeast was at the top of the comprehensive income ranking
and at the bottom of the Census money income ranking. There is also
great variability in Northeastern poverty across time—between 1985
and 1990 the Northeast falls from the top to the bottom of the regional
ranking in terms of comprehensive income. Over the entire decade, the
Northeast changed from having quite low poverty compared to other
regions, to having significantly greater poverty than the West and Midwest and the same poverty as the South. If reliable methods for correct-

Figure 5. Hesse Diagrams for Statistical Rankings of Sen Indices of Poverty by Region and Income Measures, 1979, 1985, and 1990*

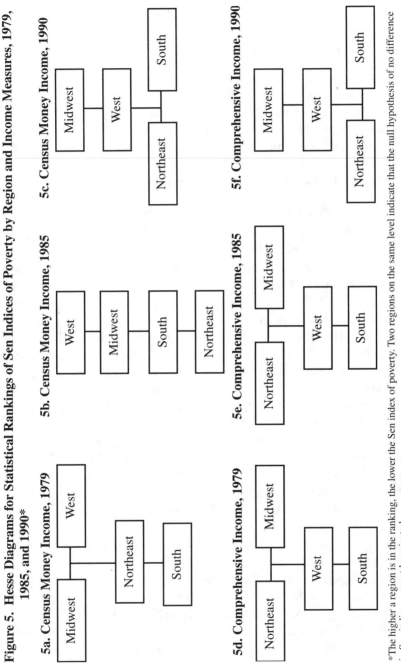

5a. Census Money Income, 1979

5b. Census Money Income, 1985

5c. Census Money Income, 1990

5d. Comprehensive Income, 1979

5e. Comprehensive Income, 1985

5f. Comprehensive Income, 1990

*The higher a region is in the ranking, the lower the Sen index of poverty. Two regions on the same level indicate that the null hypothesis of no difference in Sen indices cannot be rejected.

ing absolute incomes for differences in regional costs of living were available, then the problem of poverty in the Northeast would, in all likelihood, be revealed to be even more severe.[9]

Regional Income Inequality

Advances in the measurement of regional income inequality have been made possible by the development of statistical inference procedures for Lorenz dominance. The original test procedure was proposed by Beach and Davidson (1983), with important improvements and extensions by Beach and Kalisky (1986) and Bishop, Formby, and Thistle (1989). The new methods have been applied to large samples drawn from the public use computer files of the Census of Population and used by Bishop, Formby and Thistle (1992, 1994) to measure U.S. regional income inequality. As noted above, the use of micro data allows the income receiving unit to be defined in alternative ways and the results reported below are for three widely used definitions: the household, which is the basic sampling unit in income surveys; per capita household; and "needs-adjusted" equivalent persons per household, with the latter based upon the equivalence scale implicit in the Orshansky poverty thresholds.[10] Bishop, Formby and Thistle present results for the South and non-South (1992) and for major regions (1994) in 1969 and 1979. Figure 6 summarizes their findings in a Hesse diagram that shows the statistical rankings. Figure 6a indicates that in 1969 there were no statistically significant differences among the Lorenz curves of the major regions comprising the non-South, and all three non-South regions Lorenz dominated the South. Thus, regional differences in inequality in 1969 represented a continuation of the historical pattern that prevailed throughout much of the nineteenth and twentieth centuries. In the 1970s, fundamental changes occurred in the regional income distributions of the United States that resulted in convergence of the South's Lorenz curve to the rest of the country.[11] Using a confidence level of 99 percent, Bishop, Formby and Thistle (1992) show that the null hypothesis of no difference between the Lorenz curves of the South and non-South[12] cannot be rejected for any of the definitions of the income-receiving unit.[13] The convergence of the South's Lorenz curve to the Lorenz curve of the rest of the country

Figure 6. Hesse Diagrams for Statistical Rankings of Regional Lorenz Curves for Three Definitions of the Income Receiving Unit

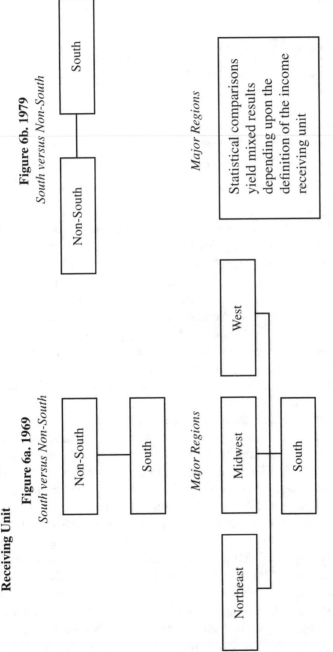

Figure 6a. 1969
South versus Non-South

Figure 6b. 1979
South versus Non-South

Major Regions

Statistical comparisons yield mixed results depending upon the definition of the income receiving unit

Major Regions

*The three definitions of the recipient unit are the household, per capita household, and "needs adjusted" equivalent number of persons per household, where the equivalence scale implicit in the Orshansky poverty thresholds are used to determine needs.

is indicated by the equivalence of the South and non-South at the top of figure 6b.

In a second study, Bishop, Formby, and Thistle (1994) decompose the non-South into the component subregions and show that while the South was *converging* to the non-South, which is an aggregation of the Northeast, Midwest and West, the regions of the non-South were *diverging* from one another. The Lorenz curves of the major regions in 1979 are sensitive to the definition of the income-receiving unit and are not easily described with a Hesse diagram. Nevertheless, several interesting results reported by Bishop, Formby and Thistle (1994) are worth noting. First, for household Lorenz curves, there are statistically significant differences between component regions of the non-South in 1979. There are also no differences in inequality between the South, Midwest and West. However, the Midwest Lorenz dominates the South. Second, for per capita incomes, the Northeast and West Lorenz curves appear to have been equivalent. But the Midwest dominates the Northeast and South and is dominated by the West. For the needs-adjusted Lorenz curves, the pattern of regional inequality in 1979 is even more complex. Pairwise Lorenz comparisons of the West and South, Midwest and Northeast and Midwest, and West and Northeast suggest equivalent needs-adjusted relative inequality. However, the inference tests indicate that in 1979, the needs-adjusted Lorenz curve of the West dominated the Midwest, while the South was dominated by both Midwest and Northeast.

The changes in regional income inequality in the 1970s were dramatic and lead to the natural question of what factors account for the observed patterns. Economists have been expecting and predicting the convergence of the South and non-South for a long time, but the diverging income distributions in the regions of the non-South are more difficult to explain. The integration of labor and capital markets and the free flow of resources between the North and the South tends to lead to equalization of factor prices and income in the long run. Thus, it is scarcely surprising that the South finally converged or almost converged to the rest of the United States. It is more difficult to explain why the income distributions of the Northeast, Midwest, and West diverged in the 1970s. Bishop, Formby and Thistle (1994) offer a tentative explanation of this surprising development. They suggest that the 1970s was a period of disequilibrium in terms of regional income distributions that reflected a more open U.S. economy and international trade, rising relative prices of energy, rapid technological change, and massive flows of highly educated and skilled workers out of the Northeast and, to a certain extent the Midwest, to the South and West. If this explanation is correct, it is reasonable to expect the regions of the non-South to eventually converge so that they are again statistically equivalent when evaluated in terms of Lorenz dominance.

Regional inequality in the 1980s and 1990s has not been studied with the same intensity as the 1960s and 1970s, and Bishop, Formby and Thistle's work has not been replicated for the more recent period. However, Bishop, Formby and Smith (1992) have applied the same inference-based Lorenz dominance methodology to annual CPS survey data and documented a massive rise in overall U.S. income inequality during the period 1978 to 1983. Relative inequality continued to rise in the United States as a whole into the late 1980s, but recently the rise seems to have abated. When regional inequality during this period is studied, it will be surprising if the unprecedented increases in the late 1970s and 1980s did not also involve significant regional changes in inequality.

Conclusions and Policy Implications

Since the early work of Watts (1968), it has been recognized that poverty is a multidimensional concept, and that the social and economic problems associated with it do not disappear when one crosses a particular income line. Nevertheless, economic definitions and measurement are essential if we are to understand poverty and be in a position to evaluate policy proposals that influence the well-being of a large segment of our population. The work of philosopher John Rawls (1971) would have us evaluate the well-being of an entire society by focusing on the poorest individual. Many people are probably unwilling to accept Rawls' stringent criterion; a proposition that would likely garner more widespread support among most Americans is that when poverty significantly increases, there can be no claim of an overall improvement in the economy even if the average income rises or the middle class benefits. Further, many would accept the proposition that substantial and rising disparities in poverty across regions and among other population subgroups is another relevant dimension along which the overall well-being of a society can be judged.

If the last two propositions are accepted as axioms for use in evaluating policy proposals, then they have immediate implications for welfare reform, middle class tax cuts, and the proposal to end unfunded federal mandates to state governments that is being widely discussed in Washington at the present time. Many Americans perceive that the system of public welfare jointly administered by states and the federal government is in need of reform, and over the last several years a new political coalition has emerged and it now seems possible that substantial changes will be enacted. Both major political parties have legislative plans to reduce transfers to the poor and use the proceeds to fund a revenue neutral tax to what is variously described as the "middle class." Further, the President is committed to "ending welfare as we know it" and to a middle class tax cut. In addition, there is a major push that has strong bipartisan support to end unfunded federal mandates to state governments. Thus, the mid 1990s seem to be a period in which Director's Law of Income Redistribution is likely to apply with a vengeance. Director's Law (Stigler 1970) holds that political competition for the support of the middle class will lead democratic governments to redistribute income to families in the middle of the income distribution. In principle, the Law is symmetrical with respect to persons in the upper and lower tails of the distribution, but today those who appear most likely to lose from the operation of Director's Law are welfare recipients at the bottom of the income distribution.

Regardless of the intent of the proposed policy shifts and irrespective of the long-run effects of such changes on welfare dependency, there are short-run impact effects of the policies currently being discussed that are not well understood and which have important implications for economic well-being. When Sen proposed his poverty index in 1976, he observed that measures of poverty that emphasized only the poverty line and the headcount ratio provided policy makers with the option of playing games; they can implement policies that they can claim make things better, while in fact they are making them worse. Suppose the policy makers are interested in headlines and 30-second sound bites and are in fact seeking to get reelected by implementing

Director's Law. What are they likely to do? It seems that they will do pretty much what Sen anticipated.

I want to conclude with the description of a simple simulation to investigate the redistributive effects of welfare reform. In 1994 I began working on the relationship of the food stamp program to poverty and have a very nice data set on comprehensive incomes and food stamps. In order to gauge the effects of reforming the food stamp program, I simulated the effects of cutting this aspect of the welfare program. Revenue saved by cutting food stamps was statistically redistributed in a revenue-neutral manner by lowering middle class tax rates. Cuts of 25 percent, 50 percent, 75 percent, and 100 percent were simulated, which generated quite a lot of revenue to finance redistributions to the middle class. What impact would cuts of this magnitude have on poverty? If only the official poverty statistics are considered, the answer is nothing; food stamps are not counted as a part of Census money income. On the other hand, if the official poverty line and measurement methodology are applied to comprehensive income, the simulations suggest that headcount poverty increases only slightly, but the poverty gap, the Gini index among the poor and the Sen index all rise substantially more. The simulations suggest the following effects of completely eliminating the food stamp program:

Census Money Income	
Official Poverty Statistics	No Change

Comprehensive Income	
Headcount Poverty Rate	+ 7.9%
Poverty (Income) Gap Ratio	+13.3%
Gini Index of the Poor	+13.5%
Sen Index of Poverty	+20.2%

These simulations strongly suggest that, if enacted, the current policy proposals will seriously aggravate the problem of poverty in America. If the axioms advanced above are accepted, then the short-run impacts of welfare reform policies will be to lower the overall economic well-being of the country.

I now conclude by pointing out that I have not simulated the effects of welfare reform on regional poverty or on other population sub-groups, but the short-run impacts are predictable. Overall, poverty will rise and poverty among vulnerable groups such as children is likely to rise substantially more than the average. Reforming the food stamp and the AFDC program are likely to have a quite different regional impact on poverty. The reason for this is that the size of AFDC payments varies widely from state to state; the maximum payments are generally much smaller in the South than in the non-South. For example, in 1991, Alabama's maximum AFDC payment for a family of three was $124, whereas Michigan's maximum was $555. Clearly, federal cuts in AFDC would be much more severe in the non-South. In contrast, food stamps are allocated on the basis of Census money income, and there is much less regional variation. But even in the case of food stamp reform, I expect that there will be significant differences in the regional impacts of welfare reform.

NOTES

1. Smolensky, Danziger and Gottschalk (1988) apply the Orshansky measurement procedures to samples drawn from the 1940 and 1950 decennial Census of Population, which contains income data for 1939 and 1949. The measurement procedures cannot be replicated exactly, but their estimates indicate that 68.1 percent of Americans were poor in 1939, and 39.7 percent were in poverty in 1949.

2. The incidence of poverty among children has been rising more rapidly than in the general population. On this point see Smolensky, Danziger and Gottschalk (1988).

3. Other data sources could be used but they involve either much smaller samples or they are not truly representative of the regional populations of interest.

4. The Lorenz curve for 1949 in figure 3a crosses the Lorenz curve for 1989 in figure 3b.

5. Census money income includes wages and salaries + self-employment income + dividends, rents, and interest + cash transfers.

6. See, for example, Braun (1988).

7. See Davies and Hoy (1994) and Formby and Zheng (1994) for discussions of this issue and the improved procedures.

8. Surveys containing more than one observation of income in two or more time periods are said to contain "panel data," which means the researcher can use alternative accounting periods for measuring income, poverty, and inequality. The March CPS survey contains observations for two consecutive years for approximately one-half the households surveyed each year. The Survey of Income and Program Participation (SIPP) contains thirty monthly observations, which means the accounting period can vary from one month up to 2.5 years. The Consumer Expenditure Survey contains quarterly data for five quarters. The longest panels that are broadly representative of the entire population are Panel Survey of Income Dynamics (PSID) and the Internal Revenue Service's continuous Work History File, which contain annual income observations for extended time periods.

9. Variations in the regional cost of living are widely recognized to be a problem when poverty is measured using absolute incomes. See, for example, the General Accounting Office's *Federal Aid: Revising Poverty Statistics Affects Fairness of Allocation Formulas* (1994). Unfortunately, there are no consistent and reliable measures of differences in regional cost of living across time. A number of researchers including Tremblay (1986) and Bishop, Formby, and Thistle (1992, 1994) have used the Bureau of Labor Statistics' *Three Budgets for an Urban Family of Four Persons* (U.S. Department of Labor 1979) to construct valid regional cost of living indices for the 1960s and 1970s. Unfortunately, a key statistical series required to estimate regional costs of living using this methodology was discontinued by the Bureau of Labor Statistics in response to Reagan administration budget cuts in the early 1980s.

10. Cowell (1984) reviews alternative definitions of the income-receiving unit and suggests criteria for limiting the number considered. The three definitions considered correspond to the approaches he most strongly recommends. It is worth pointing out that all adjustment of the micro data to obtain alternative recipient units are completed prior to grouping the data into deciles and conducting statistical tests. For example, a four-person household with total income of $30,000 is included in the per capita household income-receiving unit as four separate incomes of $7,500 each. For a four-person household, the Orshansky needs index is 1.95 and four needs-adjusted incomes of $15,384.62 are included in the needs-adjusted equivalent person income distribution.

11. There is a growing literature on regional convergence that focuses on absolute incomes. See, for example, Barro and Sala-i-Martin (1991, 1992), who focus on regional growth and the convergence of per capita mean incomes. Bishop, Formby, and Thistle (1992, 1994) analyze convergence of entire income distributions and consider both absolute and relative incomes.

12. Micro data allow the regions to be defined by a combination of states. To enhance the comparability of their results, Bishop, Formby, and Thistle (1992) use the Census definitions of the South, which includes AL, AR, DE, FL,GA,KY, LA, MD, MS,NC, OK, SC, TN, TX, VA, WV, and Washington, DC. The remaining contiguous states make up the non-South.

13. This result is sensitive to the confidence level of the test. If a 5 percent test is used, convergence is complete for the per capita and needs-adjusted Lorenz curves. However, the Lorenz curve of household income, the south had not quite converged in the bottom decile. On this point, see Bishop, Formby, and Thistle (1992).

References

Atkinson, Anthony B. 1970. "On the Measurement of Inequality," *Journal of Economic Theory* (September): 244-263.

Barro, Robert J., and Xavier Sala-i-Martin. 1991. "Convergence across States and Regions," *Brookings Papers on Economic Activity* 1: 107-182.

_____. 1992. "Convergence," *Journal of Political Economy* (April): 223-251.

Beach, Charles M., and Russell Davidson. 1983. "Distribution-Free Statistical Tests for Income Shares and Lorenz Curves," *Review of Economic Studies* (October): 723-734.

_____. 1985. "Joint Confidence Intervals for Income Shares and Lorenz Curves," *International Economic Review* (June): 439-450.

Beach, Charles M., and Stephen F. Kaliski. 1986. "Lorenz Curve Inference with Sample Weights: An Application to the Distribution of Unemployment Experience," *Applied Statistics* 1: 38-45.

Bishop, John A., John P. Formby, and W. James Smith. 1991. "Lorenz Dominance and Welfare: Changes in the U.S. Distribution of Income, 1967-1986," *Review of Economics and Statistics* (February): 134-139.

Bishop, John A., John P. Formby, and Paul D. Thistle. 1989. "Statistical Inference, Income Distribution and Social Welfare." In *Research on Economic Inequality,* Vol. 1, Daniel J. Slottje, ed. Greenwich, CN: JAI Press.

_____. 1992. "Convergence of the South and Non-South Income Distributions, 1969-1979," *American Economic Review* (March): 262-272.

_____. 1994. "Convergence and Divergence of Regional Income Distributions and Welfare," *Review of Economics and Statistics* (May): 228-235.

Bishop, John A., John P. Formby, and Buhong Zheng. 1994. "Inference Tests for Sen's Poverty Index with an Application to Regional Poverty in the United States." Working Paper No. 240, University of Alabama.

Braun, Denny. 1988. "Multiple Measures of U.S. Income Inequality," *Review of Economics and Statistics* (August): 398-405.

Cowell, Frank. 1984. "The Structure of American Income Inequality," *Review of Income and Wealth* (September): 351-375.

Davies, James, and Michael Hoy. 1994. "Making Inequality Comparisons When Lorenz Curves Intersect," *American Economic Review* (May): 980-986.

Formby, John P., and Buhong Zheng. 1994. "Unanimous Inequality Rankings and Normalized Stochastic Dominance." Working Paper No. 239, University of Alabama.

Orshansky, Mollie. 1964. "Counting the Poor: Another Look at the Poverty Profile," *Social Security Bulletin* (June): 387-406.

Rawls, John. 1971. *A Theory of Justice.* Cambridge, MA: Harvard University Press.

Sen, Amartya K. 1976. "Poverty: An Ordinal Approach to Measurement," *Econometrica* (March): 219-231.

Smolensky, Eugene, Sheldon Danziger, and Peter Gottschalk. 1988. "The Declining Significance of Age in the United States: Trends in the Well-Being of Children and the Elderly Since 1939." In *The Vulnerable,* John L. Palmer, Timothy Smeeding, and Barbara Boyle Torrey, eds. Washington DC: Urban Institute Press.

Stigler, G. 1970. "Director's Law of Public Income Redistribution," *Journal of Law and Economics* (April): 1-10.

Tremblay, Carol H. 1986. "Regional Wage Differentials: Has the South Risen Again?" *Review of Economics and Statistics* (February): 175-178.

Watts, Harold. 1968. "An Economic Definition of Poverty." In *On Understanding Poverty,* Daniel P. Moynihan, ed. New York: Basic Books.

Williamson, Jeffrey G. 1977. "Unbalanced Growth, Inequality, and Regional Development: Some Lessons from U.S. History." In *Alternatives to Confrontation: A National Policy Toward Regional Change,* V.L. Arnold, ed. Lexington, MA: Lexington Books.

Wright, Gavin. 1987. "The Economic Revolution in the American South," *Journal of Economic Perspectives* (Summer): 161-178.

U.S. Department of Labor. 1979. *Three Budgets for an Urban Family of Four Persons,* Washington DC: Bureau of Labor Statistics.

U.S. General Accounting Office. 1994. "Federal Aid: Revising Poverty Statistics Affects Fairness of Allocation Formulas." GAO, Washington, DC.

U.S. Bureau of the Census. 1981. "Characteristics of the Population Below the Poverty Level: 1979," by Carol Fendler and Arno I. Winard. *Current Population Reports,* series P-60, No. 130. Washington, DC: U.S. Government Printing Office.

_____. 1990. "Poverty in the United States: 1988 and 1989," by Mark S. Littman and Eleanor F. Baugher. *Current Population Reports,* series P-60, No. 171. Washington, DC: U.S. Government Printing Office.

_____. 1993. "Poverty in the United States: 1992," by Eleanor F. Baugher and Martina Shea. *Current Population Reports,* series P-60, No. 185. Washington, DC.: U.S. Government Printing Office.

The International Evidence on Income Distribution in Modern Economics
Where Do We Stand?

Timothy M. Smeeding
Syracuse University
and
Luxembourg Income Study

Interest in cross-national comparison of personal income distributions, low relative incomes, and income inequality in general has grown dramatically during the past several years. Interest in cross-national distribution research did not come about by accident; several factors helped propel this line of research in the 1980s and 1990s. First of all, income distributions in the United States, the United Kingdom, and in several other nations began to trend toward greater inequality. Second, the former socialist nations of Central and Eastern Europe (CEE) began a still-continuing process of economic and social adjustment and transition to a new socioeconomic order. While this transition is still underway, CEE nations have experienced large changes in both real income levels and in income distribution. Third, along with the rise in inequality, a growing interest in the question of "fairness pressures" was present in the national political debates of the late 1980s and early 1990s, thus making "income distribution" a legitimate realm of political inquiry.[1] Finally, the emergence of comparable cross-national data on distribution allowed for comparisons of similarities and differences across countries and over time. Similarities and differences in experiences may help us understand how market forces, demographic trends, and public policy affect the relative economic status of various groups in each nation.

This chapter summarizes and provides limited updates on a small part of what was learned in a large study undertaken for the OECD (Atkinson, Rainwater, and Smeeding 1995a), and a subsequent review article (Gottschalk and Smeeding 1996). It also adds recent material for CEE nations (Torrey, Smeeding, and Bailey 1996) and for Taiwan (Republic of China).

The chapter starts from a position of caution as to what can be achieved by a summary of the empirical evidence. Due to space constraints, we are unable to enumerate all of the limitations of the data. However, we should note that the quality of the CEE datasets is questionable, since we have not been able to verify their data by comparing them with administrative records. On the other hand, the data for OECD nations is generally high quality. All of these data were generated by the Luxembourg Income Study, and those interested in this dataset should consult Atkinson, Rainwater, and Smeeding (1995a, chapters 2, 3, and appendices).

Of course, the quality of the data is not the only reason for exercising caution in drawing conclusions regarding recent trends in inequality. The problem of choosing a measure of inequality is also troublesome, as is the even more basic problem of measuring income. The section that follows contains an introduction to those measures of inequality most commonly taken, as well as definitions of income. Throughout this paper we concentrate our attention on inequality in only two measures of income: market income and disposable income.[2]

The degree of income inequality in the 1980s and early 1990s is then compared among twenty-five countries. These are the eighteen OECD nations, five eastern European nations, and Israel and Taiwan. One question to be asked is whether one can identify distinct groupings of countries with different degrees of inequality? A brief discussion of the trend in inequality in recent years follows, asking if there is a worldwide trend toward greater inequality or whether groups of countries have had similar experiences. Some of the factors that seem to have affected inequality are addressed, including differences in market incomes, demographic factors, and government intervention (direct taxes and transfers). The final section summarizes the chapter and offers suggestions for additional research.

Choices and Measures

There are currently no international standards for income distribution that parallel the international standards used for systems of national income accounts.[3] Hence, researchers need to decide what they want to measure and how far they can measure it on a comparable basis. The Luxembourg Income Study offers the researcher many choices of perspective in terms of country, income measure, accounting unit, and time frame, but its relatively short time frame (1979-1993 for most nations, but 1968-1995 for five countries) and limited number of observation periods per country (three to five periods per country at present) currently limits its usefulness for studying longer term trends in income distribution. The purpose of this section of the paper is to explain the choices we have made in our use of the Luxembourg Income Study.

Choices: Inequality of What among Whom on What Terms?

Our attention is focussed primarily on the distribution of *disposable money income*, that is income after direct taxes plus transfer payments. Several points should be noted:

1. Income rather than consumption is taken as the indicator of resources, although there may be both theoretical and empirical arguments favoring use of the latter.

2. The definition of income falls considerably short of the Haig-Simons comprehensive definition, typically excluding much of capital gains, imputed rents, home production, and most of income in-kind (with the exception of near-cash benefits).

3. No account is taken of indirect taxes or of the benefits from public spending (other than cash and near-cash transfers) such as health care, education, or most housing subsidies.

4. The period of income measurement is in general the calendar year, with income measured on an annual basis (although the United Kingdom evidence relates to weekly or monthly income).

Thus, variables measured may be less than ideal, and results may not be fully comparable across countries. For example, one country may help low-income families through money benefits (included in cash income), whereas another provides subsidized housing, child care, or education (which are not taken into account). While, a recent study (Smeeding et al. 1993) finds that the distribution of housing, education, and health care benefits reinforces the general differences in income distribution for a subset of the western nations examined here, there is no guarantee that these relationships hold for other countries or methods of accounting.[4] Still this study shows that countries that spend more for cash benefits tend also to spend more for noncash benefits. Because noncash benefits are more equally distributed than are cash benefits, levels of inequality within countries are lessened, but the same rank ordering of these countries with respect to inequality levels found here using cash alone persists when noncash benefits are added in.

Market income, which includes earned income from wages and salaries and self-employment, cash property income (but not capital gains or losses), and other private cash income transfers (occupational pensions, alimony, and child support) is the primary source of disposable income for most nonelderly families. To obtain disposable income, we first add public transfer payments (social retirement, family allowances, unemployment compensation, welfare benefits) and deduct personal income tax and social security contributions from market income. Then near-cash benefits—those that are virtually equivalent to cash (food stamps in the United States and housing allowances in the United Kingdom and Sweden)—are added in.[5] Thus, differences between disposable and market income capture the net effects of income redistribution.

The question of the distribution "amongst whom" is here given the simplest answer: amongst individuals. When assessing disposable income inequality, however, the unit of aggregation is the household: the incomes of all household members are aggregated and then divided by an equivalence scale to arrive at individual equivalent income. The choice of the household, rather than a narrower unit such as the spending unit or the family, is open to debate. It captures the economies of scale extant in shared living arrangements, but it assumes a degree of income-sharing within the household that may not be realized.[6]

Data Base

The aim of the Luxembourg Income Study data used here is to increase the degree of cross-national comparability, but complete cross-national comparability is not possible, even if we were to administer our own surveys in each nation. Comparability is a matter of degree, and all that one can hope for is to reach an acceptably high level. It is left to the reader to decide if the level of comparability found in this study is acceptable. Many of the cross-national results provided here have been reviewed by a team of national experts—statisticians, social scientists, and policy analysts—prior to their publication by OECD and in other forums. This painstaking two-year process helped improve the quality of the analysis while also testing the mettle of both the analysts and the reviewers. In some nations, we only update OECD results to a later year using the same national database. Finally, our results for CEE nations have been reviewed by teams of country experts, but not by national authorities.

Income Inequality in Twenty-Five Nations

The Luxembourg Income Study data sets have been used here to compare the distribution of disposable income in twenty-five nations over a five- to ten-year period.[7] The numbers presented are taken from the most recent LIS data and correspond generally to the results found in Atkinson, Rainwater, and Smeeding (1995a), which use earlier years' LIS data in most cases. Table 1 gives the incomes of high- and low-income persons as percentages of median income. High income (P90) is defined as the income of a person in the 90th percentile of the income distribution while low income is that of a person in the 10th percentile.[8] The ratio of high-to-low incomes (decile ratio) is also shown. For instance, the high-to-low ratio in Russia is 6.83, indicating that a person with an income at the 90th percentile enjoys almost seven times the income of a person at the 10th percentile. This is the highest decile ratio in our sample, followed by the United States (5.67) and Australia (4.26).

**Table 1. The Gap between Low- and High-Income Individuals
(numbers given are percent in each nation)**

Country	Low[a]	High[b]	Ratio of high to low[c]
Slovak Republic 1992	66	149	2.25
Czech Republic 1992	65	155	2.36
Finland 1991	58	158	274
Belgium 1992	59	163	2.76
Sweden 1992	58	159	2.77
Norway 1991	57	158	2.79
Denmark 1992	55	155	2.84
Netherlands 1991	59	172	2.94
Germany 1984	57	170	2.98
Luxembourg 1985	59	184	3.12
Italy 1991	56	176	3.14
Austria 1987	56	187	3.34
Switzerland 1982	54	185	3.43
Hungary 1991	53	180	3.46
New Zealand 1987/88	54	187	3.46
France 1984	55	193	3.51
Poland 1992	51	192	3.76
United Kingdom 1986	51	194	3.80
Canada 1991	47	183	3.86
Republic of China/Taiwan 1991	50	195	3.90
Spain 1990	49	198	4.04
Ireland 1987	50	209	4.18
Australia 1989	45	193	4.26
United States 1991	37	207	5.67
Russia 1992	35	239	6.83
Average[d]	53	182	3.53

SOURCE: Author's tabulation of data in the Luxembourg Income Study.
a. Relative income for individuals who are lower than 90 percent of the individuals in the country and higher than 10 percent of the individuals as a percent of national median.
b. Relative income for individuals who are higher than 90 percent of the individuals in the country and lower than 10 percent of the individuals as a percent of national median.
c. Ratio of 90th to 10th percentiles, or decile ratio.
d. Simple 25-nation average.

Looking at the low column in table 1, we see that the three countries with the highest decile ratio are characterized by low P10 values. In Russia, the United States, and Australia, the relative incomes of persons in the 10th percentile are 35, 37, and 45 respectively. These are the lowest values in our sample, and contrast with values ranging from 52 to 60 for countries with a below-average decile ratio. However, countries with above-average decile ratios also tend to have high incomes substantially greater than average. In fact, though Russia, the United States, and Australia are distinguished by high incomes well above the average for the sample, other high-decile ratio countries—such as Ireland, Spain, and Taiwan—have very respectable low-income levels (50, 49, 50).

While percentile ratios have some obvious appeal (e.g., insensitivity to top coding, ease of understanding), they have the disadvantage of focusing on only a few points in the distribution and lack a normative basis. Table 2 presents an alternative Lorenz-based summary measure of inequality, the Gini coefficient, with countries grouped according to type (OECD, CEE, Taiwan, Israel).[9]

Among the OECD nations, the lowest Gini is found in Finland, followed by most but not all of the Scandinavian nations. Austria's coefficients must be treated with caution because of their exclusion of self-employment income, but they and those of the smallest Benelux nations come next, followed by West Germany, Italy, and the Netherlands. There is then a gap of 0.15 points to Canada and France. The United Kingdom, Spain, and Australia are next, with another gap of 0.14 to Switzerland, Ireland, and finally the United States. As measured by these Ginis, the range of inequality across OECD nations runs from 0.223 (Finland) to 0.343 (United States), or by as much as 54 percent.

Turning to the CEE nations, income inequality in the Czech and Slovak Republics is most similar to that found in the Scandinavian economies, while Hungary and Poland are similar to France, Canada, Australia, and the United Kingdom. Russia had the highest Gini as well as the highest rich-to-poor ratio of all countries for which we have LIS data in the 1990s. This is partially the result of some very high incomes, since the Gini changes by a large fraction when we impose a top code of 10 times the median adjusted income in Russia, while other nations' estimates change little, if at all. But even when income is top-

Table 2. Measures of Inequality in OECD Countries, in Transition Economies, and in Taiwan and Israel

Country	Year	Gini (1)[a]	Gini (2)[b]
A. OECD Countries			
Finland	1991	0.223	0.223
Austria[c]	1987	0.227	0.227
Sweden	1992	0.229	0.229
Belgium	1992	0.230	0.230
Norway	1991	0.233	0.233
Luxembourg	1985	0.238	0.238
Denmark	1992	0.240	0.239
Germany (West)	1984	0.250	0.249
Italy	1991	0.255	0.255
The Netherlands	1991	0.271	0.268
Canada	1991	0.286	0.285
France	1984	0.295	0.294
United Kingdom	1986	0.304	0.303
Spain	1990	0.308	0.306
Australia	1989	0.309	0.308
Switzerland	1982	0.323	0.311
Ireland	1987	0.330	0.328
United States	1991	0.343	0.343
B. CEE Transition Countries			
Slovak Republic	1992	0.189	0.189
Czech Republic	1992	0.208	0.207
Hungary	1991	0.289	0.289
Poland	1992	0.291	0.290

Country	Year	Gini (1)[a]	Gini (2)[b]
Russia	1992	0.437	0.393
C. Taiwan and Israel			
Republic of China/Taiwan	1991	0.302	0.300
Israel	1992	0.305	0.305

SOURCE: Authors' tabulation of data in the Luxembourg Income Study.
a. Gini (1) = Gini coefficient for equivalent disposable income (EI) where $EI = DPI/S^E$. S = family size, E = 0.5, person weighted, bottom-coded at 1 percent mean DPI.
b. Gini (2) = Gini (1) top-coded at 10 times median disposable income.
c. Austria excludes the self-employed.

coded, Russia still has the highest Gini and the ranking of nations is unaffected.

Based on these data, there is a wider range of disposable income inequality in the five CEE transition countries than in the major—and much richer—OECD nations. It is interesting that Russia, the CEE nation that experienced the most rapid transition to a market economy, has the highest level of inequality, while inequality is the least in the Czech and Slovak Republics where the transition to a market economy has been considerably slower (the "velvet revolution"). Finally, the Republic of China and Israel have inequality levels near the middle of the OECD range, with Ginis very similar to that found in the United Kingdom.

The Comparative Trend in Income Inequality

In this section we lay out the facts of how income inequality has changed over the past fifteen to twenty-five years in major modern nations. Studies of the recent trends in income inequality in different nations are listed in table 3.[10] While the various studies surveyed use different income and inequality measures and cover different periods, they are sufficiently robust to paint a picture of overall changes in inequality during the 1980s and into the early 1990s in a large number of nations.[11] These series cover a reasonable time span and the data themselves are internally consistent over time. Therefore, they give an indi-

Table 3. Changes in Market and Disposable Income Inequality

Country	Source	Period	Market income inequality[a]	Disposable income inequality
United Kingdom	Goodman and Webb (1994) Atkinson (1993)	1981 - 1991	+++	++++
United States	Gottschalk and Danziger (1995) U.S. Bureau of the Census (1995, 1995a)		+++	+++
Sweden	Gustafsson and Palmer (1993)	1980 - 1992	+++	+++
Hungary	Torrey, Smeeding, and Bailey (1995)	1987 - 1992	n.a.	+++
Poland	Torrey, Smeeding, and Bailey (1995)	1987 - 1992	n.a.	++
Czech Republic	Torrey, Smeeding, and Bailey (1995)	1987 - 1992	n.a.	++
Australia	Saunders (1994)	1980 - 1989	++	++
New Zealand	Saunders (1994)	1981 - 1989	+	++
Japan	Tachabanaki and Yagi (1995) Bauer and Mason (1992)	1981 - 1990	+	++
Denmark	LIS (1996)	1987 - 1992	++	++
Slovak Republic	Torrey, Smeeding, and Bailey (1995)	1980 - 1992	n.a.	+
The Netherlands	Central Bureau of Statistics (1993) Muffells and Nellison (1993)	1981 - 1989	+	+
Norway	Epland (1992)	1982 - 1989	+	+
Belgium	Cantillon, et al. (1994)	1985 - 1992	+	+

Country	Source	Period		
Canada	Beach and Slottsve (1994) Statistics Canada	1980 - 1992	+	0
Israel	LIS (1995)	1979 - 1992	+	0
Finland	Uusitalo (1994)	1981 - 1992	+++	0
France	Concialdi (1993)	1979 - 1989	0	0
Republic of China	LIS (1995)	1981 - 1991	0	0
Portugal	Rodrigues (1993)	1980 - 1990	0	0
Spain	LIS (1995)	1980 - 1990	n.a.	0
Ireland	Callan and Nolan (1993)	1980 - 1987	+	0
West Germany	Burkhauser and Poupore (1994) Hauser and Becker (1993)	1983 - 1990	+	0
Italy	Brandolini and Sestito (1993) Erickson and Ichino (1992)	1976 - 1991	--	--

NOTE: See Smeeding and Gottschalk (1995, table A-1) for actual figures.

Designation	Interpretation	Range of change in Gini
--	small decline	-5 percent or more
0	zero	-4 to +4 percent
+	small increase	5 to 10 percent
++	Moderate increase	10 to 15 percent
+++	large increase	16 to 29 percent
++++	extremely large increase	30 percent or more

a. Some studies show changes in overall earnings inequality, others show changes in market income inequality, and still others do not discuss market income changes at all.

cation of the relative trends in different countries. Our evaluation of the magnitude and direction of these changes can be found in column five of table 3. These evaluations are based on the Gini coefficients that are used in all the studies reviewed here. Countries are listed in order of change in disposable income inequality from largest to smallest change. Where they are available from the same studies, we also present data on the trend in market income inequality in each nation.

Both the United Kingdom and the United States experienced a substantial rise in inequality during the 1980s, with the increase in the United Kingdom being much greater over this time period. Whereas trends in earnings inequality were similar in the United States and the United Kingdom, the time paths for changes in the distribution of family income were markedly different. In the United Kingdom, income inequality fell through the mid-1970s, but the Gini coefficient rose by more than 30 percent between 1978 and 1991. This is almost double the increase over two decades in the United States, and more than double the decline in the United Kingdom from 1949 to 1976.[12] In fact by 1991, the overall level of income inequality in the United Kingdom exceeded the level found in Canada, a much larger nation.

While starting from a much lower level of inequality, Sweden experienced a pattern of change in inequality similar to that in the United Kingdom, downward until 1981, then fairly level during the 1980s, with a sharp increase in the early 1990s. But though the Swedish Gini increased by about 20 percent from 1980 to 1992, the Swedish income distribution remained considerably more equal than either that of the United States or the United Kingdom.[13, 14]

The changes experienced by Hungary, the Czech Republic, and Poland—28, 14, and 12 percent respectively, over a shorter period (three and five years, respectively)—are closer to our expectations. While the Hungarian change is very large, the changes found in Poland and in the Czech Republic are not much different from that found in the United Kingdom over the 1986-1991 period or in Sweden from 1988 to 1993.

In Australia, Denmark, and Japan (and in Poland though over a shorter period), the upward trend over the 1980s is slightly less than that experienced in the United States and Sweden. The same is true in New Zealand, though all of the increases here came during the late 1980s (Saunders 1994).[15] In Belgium, the Netherlands, the Slovak

Republic, and Norway, the overall increase in inequality was about 5 percent from 1980 to 1990. In many nations—Canada, Ireland, Israel, Portugal, Taiwan, Finland, and France—there was little or no change in the 1980s and early 1990s. And income inequality actually declined slightly in Italy during the 1980s.[16]

It is also noteworthy that there appears to be no apparent relation between the *trend* over the 1980s and the *overall level* of inequality at the start of the period. Inequality has increased both in the United States, with a very high level of inequality even before the increase, and in Sweden, which started from a much lower level of inequality. Inequality has fallen in Italy, but risen greatly in the United Kingdom, with both countries occupying intermediate inequality positions in the mid-1980s (table 1).

Nor is there a consistent "group country" story. Among the Scandinavian nations, Sweden experienced a rapid rise in inequality in the early 1990s, while Finland did not. In Europe we find large secular increases in inequality in the United Kingdom, smaller increases in Denmark, Belgium, and the Netherlands, but stasis in Germany, Portugal, Ireland, and France, with secular decreases in Italy. Canada experienced only mild increases in inequality of family income while the United States experienced much larger increases despite similar market forces affecting market incomes in both countries (Hanratty and Blank 1993). And finally, if there is a regional pattern, it is to be found among the CEE nations, with inequality rising in Poland, Hungary, and the Czech Republic near the upper end of the range found in Western nations over similar periods.

Exploring Differences in Levels and Trends

The story of why we observe these differences in levels and trends in inequality is necessarily incomplete because of the confluence of market, demographic, institutional, and policy changes. The inclusion of multiple income sources received by multiple individuals thwarts attempts to identify the causal links that lead to variations across countries and over time in the distribution of total post-tax and transfer family income. There is ample evidence that family members take account of all sources of income available to the family in deciding not only how much each member might work in a market setting, but also how to structure living arrangements. Moreover, governments themselves react differently to market income changes via changes in redistribution (tax and transfer) policy, and via other policies (e.g., macroeconomic policy or micro policies such as government employment). This leads to decision-making processes that are much too complex to be treated in a unified causal framework at this time. We therefore limit ourselves to a simple descriptive exercise that focuses on the difference in inequality before and after government redistribution.

Differences in the Level of Inequality of Market Income and
  Disposable Income

Table 4 shows the Gini coefficient for market income (pre-tax and transfer), disposable income (post-tax and transfer) and the difference between these two measures of inequality. Since taxes and transfers affect economic behavior, this difference reflects the net effect of direct taxation (income and employee social security taxes) and government transfer benefits. Clearly, both coefficients vary substantially across countries. The differences between these two Ginis also fall in a wide range; the sample high of 0.245 (Sweden) is more than ten times the sample low of 0.023 (Taiwan).

Note that the disposable income Gini (DPI) is not closely related to the level of inequality in market income (MI). For example, with MI Ginis less than 0.34, Finland, Italy, and Taiwan have the least amount of inequality in market income. But, with DPI Ginis of 0.233 and 0.255 respectively, Finland and Italy have significantly less inequality in disposable income than Taiwan, whose DPI Gini (0.302) is not much less than its MI Gini (0.325). Similarly, Hungary, France, Poland, and Canada all have DPI Ginis in the 0.285 - 0.295 range, but MI Ginis that run from 0.415 to 0.470. The weak relationship between a country's DPI and MI Ginis is suggested by the scatter in figure 1 and confirmed by the low multiple correlation coefficient (0.282) of these two series.

These data suggest that there is a wide variety of experiences underlying the relationship between inequality in market income and inequality in disposable income. And although differential behavioral responses to redistribution may contribute to the range of these DPI

Table 4. Inequality in Disposable and Market Income in Twenty-Four Nations

Country	Year	Abbreviation	DPI Gini	MI Gini	Difference
Slovak Republic	1992	SR92	0.189	0.402	0.213
Czech Republic	1992	CZ92	0.208	0.411	0.203
Finland	1991	FI91	0.233	0.337	0.114
Sweden	1992	SW92	0.229	0.474	0.245
Belgium	1992	BE92	0.230	0.456	0.226
Norway	1991	NO91	0.233	0.378	0.145
Luxembourg	1985	LX85	0.238	0.380	0.142
Denmark	1992	DK92	0.240	0.430	0.191
Germany	1984	GE84	0.250	0.428	0.178
Italy	1991	IT91	0.255	0.330	0.075
The Netherlands	1991	NL91	0.271	0.414	0.143
Canada	1991	CN91	0.286	0.415	0.129
Hungary	1991	HU91	0.289	0.491	0.202
Poland	1992	PL92	0.291	0.444	0.154
France	1984	FR84	0.295	0.470	0.175
Taiwan	1991	RC91	0.302	0.325	0.023
United Kingdom	1986	UK86	0.304	0.488	0.185
Israel	1992	IS92	0.305	0.453	0.147
Spain	1990	SP90	0.308	0.429	0.121
Australia	1990	AS90	0.309	0.437	0.128
Switzerland	1982	CH82	0.323	0.406	0.083
Ireland	1987	IR87	0.330	0.503	0.174
United States	1991	US91	0.343	0.449	0.107
Russia RLMS	1992	RL92	0.440	0.542	0.102

SOURCE: Author's tabulation of Luxembourg Income Study.
NOTE: Austria is omitted because MI cannot be computed in the LIS datasets.

94

Figure 1. Market Income and Disposable Income Inequality

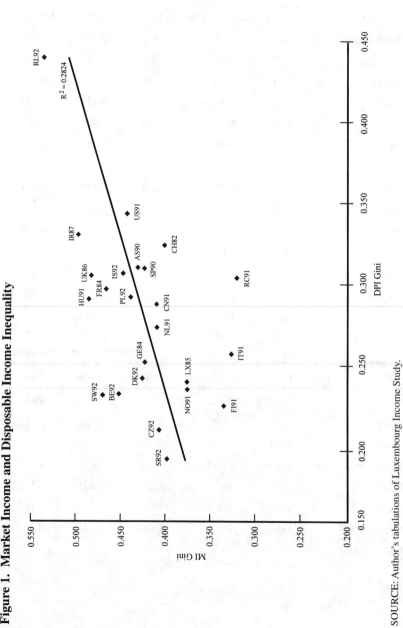

SOURCE: Author's tabulations of Luxembourg Income Study.

Ginis, we suspect that the difference between a country's MI and DPI Ginis is more likely to be a product of its redistributive policy.

Changes in Inequality Over Time

In the nations studied here, changes in earned income inequality appear to be the prime force behind changes in market income inequality during the 1980s. With earnings roughly at or above 70 percent of market income in most modern nations, this is to be expected. Other market forces along with demographic and social developments also affected market income inequality, though to a lesser degree. However, while market income changes are dominant, they do not tell the whole story. By the mid-1980s, more than 25 percent of all households in major OECD nations depended on something other than earnings as the primary source of their incomes. In nations such as the United Kingdom, the Netherlands, and Sweden, this figure reached 30 percent (Atkinson, Rainwater, and Smeeding 1995b, table 8).

The crude evidence in table 3 indicates that the trends in disposable income inequality mirror the trends in market income inequality in most nations. In thirteen of the nineteen nations in which the changes in both market and disposable income inequality have been estimated, the change in both measures of inequality has the same sign. The link between changes in tax and transfer policy and changes in the distribution of disposable income is not very well understood at this time.[17] In countries with progressive tax and transfer systems, the effect of changes in taxes paid and transfers received would largely offset the effect of any changes in market income on the distribution of disposable income. In some countries, especially Finland, but also in Israel, Spain, Ireland, Canada, and Germany, there was no appreciable increase in the inequality of disposable income. Thus, the tax and transfer systems in place in these nations, or the redistributive policies adopted in the 1980s in response to increasing inequality in market incomes, were effective in preventing rising disposable income inequality. In contrast, in six nations inequality in disposable income kept pace with inequality in market income. That the United Kingdom, New Zealand, Denmark, and Japan experienced increases in disposable income inequality that exceeded the increases in market income inequality begs the question of whether there were retrenchments in tax/transfer program progressivity over the relevant period.

Since in fifteen of the nineteen countries for which there are data, market income inequality increased during the 1980s, it seems that rising market income inequality was a problem confronted by most if not all industrialized economies. This suggests that some of the factors behind these developments are common to all these nations. Candidates for these factors might be the growing volume and importance of international trade and a more laissez faire approach to domestic economic policy.

Summary and Research Implications

The literature on cross-national levels and trends in earning and income inequality is young but growing rapidly. Concerns about earnings inequality and joblessness have moved to the top of the social policy agenda in modern OECD nations. Over the past decade, new data resources have expanded to meet these interests. While some of these permit a broad-brush overview of the field, the growing research interest in this area has spawned a large number of collaborative efforts to examine a small number of nations in much greater detail. In this paper we attempted to briefly summarize both what can be learned from the new resources such as LIS and also from the growing literature on national and cross-national trends in inequality.

We find a wide range of levels of income inequality across the twenty-five nations studied here. The range of inequality among OECD nations is very large, and the range among CEE nations appears to be larger still. Government redistribution has a measurable effect on overall income inequality, reducing market income-based measures compared to disposable income measures in every nation. However, countries with very similar disposable income inequality often have very different inequality of market income and vice versa. These differences are yet to be fully explained.

Trends in overall income inequality diverge across nations in interesting ways. One finds large increases in inequality among very different nations: two Anglo-Saxon nations (the United Kingdom and the

United States), one Scandinavian nation (Sweden), and one CEE nation (Hungary) exhibit the largest increases in measured income inequality from roughly 1980 to 1992. In contrast, other Anglo-Saxon (e.g., Canada), European (several), and Scandinavian (e.g., Finland) nations have experienced a much smaller change in inequality while some nations have shown no measurable change in inequality.

In fact, the most distinctive changes in income distribution in modern OECD nations seem to have taken place in the United Kingdom and in the United States, where there has been a hollowing out of the middle of distribution, marked by an increasing fraction of the population both in upper and lower income groups relative to overall median income. Falling real wages for low-skill, low-income families and the growth in the number of females heading families juxtaposed against rising wages for well-educated men and women and assortative mating were the primary factors accounting for the increase in inequality in the United States.[18] In the United Kingdom, while real earnings still grew at the bottom of the earnings distribution, unemployment and rising numbers of single parents were important in building a large group at the bottom of the distribution. At the other end of the British income distribution, higher earnings for well-educated men and women, rising income from financial capital, and self-employment income all play a significant role in explaining the growing income share of high-income people. However, while the hollowing out or polarization of distributions in the United States and the United Kingdom is clear, these same patterns are not obvious in other OECD or LIS countries.[19]

Additional research is needed to further investigate the patterns found here to provide a better overall theory of income distribution. Comparisons of real income differences across countries are also instructive. Such comparisons as these, while difficult to make, can add a great deal in cases where one wishes to compare nations with similar overall levels of production and economic output (per capita GDP) to one another (see Smeeding and Gottschalk 1995). We also need to build better structural models of income distribution and redistribution that can be applied across and within nations. Atkinson's (1994) self-characterization of his review of the economic theory of income distribution is "a prospectus for a yet-unwritten book rather than a self-contained essay," a statement that I heartily endorse.

NOTES

I would like to thank, without implication, colleagues who have contributed to my work in this area: Anthony B. Atkinson, Peter Gottschalk, Lee Rainwater, Barbara Torrey, and Debra Bailey. I thank Jon Neill for editorial assistance. I would also like to thank Esther Gray, Ann Wicks, Inge O'Connor, and Debra Bailey for assistance in preparing this manuscript. Finally, I am grateful for financial support provided by the Russell Sage Foundation and by the National Science Foundation under #SBR-9022192, and #SBR-9511521. I retain responsibility for all errors of omission or commission.

1. In Scandinavia and Europe, the debate is about jobs and income support levels that are producing record budget deficits. In the United States, United Kingdom, and Canada, the debate is about budget deficits and fairness.

2. In order to realize the full range of choices and their potential applications, the larger studies need to be consulted (Atkinson, Rainwater, and Smeeding 1995a, chapters 2, 3, and appendices 2-6; Gottschalk and Smeeding 1995). In order to expand the realm of inquiry to wealth or to consumption, other sources need to be consulted (e.g., Wolff 1994, 1995; Hagenaars, deVos, and Zaidi 1994; Deaton and Paxson 1994). Moreover, the range of nations studied is confined to those for which we have data that have attained a reasonable level of comparability. Many CEE nations and Asian nations are not covered here. For additional information on their experiences, see Milanovic (1995) and Birdsall, Ross, and Sabot (1995).

3. For a discussion of the problems of comparability across countries, see, among others, Atkinson, Rainwater, and Smeeding (1995a); Buhmann et al. (1988); Smeeding, Rainwater, and O'Higgins (1990). The issue of international standards for income distribution studies is also being addressed by the Luxembourg Income Study Project.

4. Smeeding et al. (1993) covers Australia, Canada, West Germany, United Kingdom, the Netherlands, and United States around 1980.

5. In many CEE nations we have the option of adding production for own consumption (mainly among rural farm families), the value of goods produced and bartered, and in-kind transfers (food, appliances, etc.) received from outside the household. However, these amounts are not included here.

6. Our comparisons of income distribution, and of the effect of taxes and transfers on inequality, use equivalence scales to adjust families for differences in economic need as reflected by family size. These scales have been found to systematically affect the level of overall inequality, but not its pattern. See Atkinson, Rainwater, and Smeeding (1995a, chapter 4). See also Buhmann et al. (1988).

7. We compare incomes by considering household disposable income (or market income) per equivalent adult, using an "intermediate" equivalence scale of household size raised to the power of a half (or S^E where E = .5). Thus, adjusted income equals unadjusted income divided by S^E. Many recent cross-national studies of inequality and poverty have used this value for E (Atkinson, Rainwater, and Smeeding 1995; Hagenaars, deVos, and Zaidi 1994; Förster, 1993, 1994.)

8. Two sets of figures are presented, one bottom-coded at 1 percent of median disposable income, the other top-coded at 10 times median income.

9. Atkinson, Rainwater, and Smeeding (1995a, chapter 4) also present alternative summary index measures of inequality (the Atkinson ratio), and measures of Lorenz-dominance.

10. These trends are drawn from the primary studies shown in table 3 and summarized numerically in Smeeding and Gottschalk (1995, table A-1). Table A-1 also allows the reader to make longer-term comparisons of inequality for nations with such data.

11. It should be emphasized that these figures are not comparable across countries. One can draw no conclusions from these estimates about the relative degree of inequality in different countries. In each case, the estimates are drawn from national studies of income inequality that are not designed for purposes of international comparison, and they are not necessarily based on the same concepts of income or method of calculation. See Smeeding and Gottschalk (1995, table A-1) for additional details. While we have used the LIS data for inequality comparisons across a subset of these nations where other national studies are not available, the LIS data are less complete in terms of years studied than are those from the other national studies cited here. Where LIS trend data is available, however, it supports the findings shown in table 3.

12. See Atkinson (1993, table 1) and also Goodman and Webb (1994), who report similar results.

13. We have several sources of information on the trend in Swedish income inequality, including Gustafsson and Palmer (1993) and Bjorklund and Freeman (1994). The former show large increases in the Gini, particularly in 1990 and 1991. The latter appear to show a smaller increase in inequality using data through 1992, but do not use Ginis and compute only subgroup inequality trends, excluding the aged and persons aged 18 and 19. Gini estimates provided directly by Kjell Jansson of Statistics Sweden indicate that the trend in overall inequality is similar to that shown in Gustafsson and Palmer (1993).

14. Were we to show not *percentage change* but *percentage point change* in inequality, Sweden may fare a bit better than shown here. A 15 percentage point change in the Swedish 1991 Gini of 0.229 or 0.034, is less than a 10 percent change in the U.S. 1991 Gini of 0.343.

15. While the Polish data are consistent from 1987 through 1992, it is not entirely clear that the Polish household budget survey has adequately captured changes in entrepreneurial incomes since 1990. Thus, the Polish results must be cautiously interpreted.

16. Gardiner (1993) goes back further than we, to the 1980s, noting a "U"-shaped pattern of inequality change in the United States, the United Kingdom, Japan, and the Netherlands, thus capturing the decrease in inequality that occurred in the 1960s and early 1970s in these nations.

17. This conclusion draws heavily on Gottschalk and Smeeding (1996), who in turn base their conclusions on material from Gottschalk, Gustafsson, and Palmer (1995), OECD (1994), Gardiner (1993), Ploug and Kvist (1994), Messere (1994), and Commission of the European Community (1993a, 1993b).

18. The extent to which real incomes have actually fallen among American families and the amount of that decrease depends on the measure and on the time period. Depending on the period chosen, the decrease has been large (e.g., substantial declines by 40 percent of persons from 1973 to 1994 according to Karoly 1995) or small (e.g., very small declines for less than 25 percent of persons from 1979 to 1989 according to Burkhauser et al. 1996). Still the large majority of the real income gains in America during the 1980s and 1990s have gone to those at or near the top of the income distribution.

19. See Beach and Slottsve (1994) and Foster and Wolfson (1994) on Canada; for the United Kingdom see Jenkins (1994); and for the United States see U.S. Bureau of the Census (1995) and Duncan, Smeeding, and Rodgers (1994). Recent analyses using the LIS database also fail to find such a pattern in any other modern OECD nation through 1992.

References

Atkinson, A.B. 1993. "What is Happening to the Distribution of Income in the U.K.?" *Proceedings of the British Academy* 82: 317-351.

_____. 1994. "Explaining the Distribution of Income." Mimeo prepared for the J. Roundtree Inquiry into Income and Wealth, University of Cambridge.

Atkinson, A.B., L. Rainwater, and T. Smeeding. 1995a. *Income Distribution in OECD Countries: Evidence from the Luxembourg Income Study (LIS).* Paris: OECD, October.

_____. 1995b. "Income Distribution in Advanced Economies: Evidence from the Luxembourg Income Study." LIS-CEPS Working Paper No. 120.

Bauer, J., and A. Mason. 1992. "The Distribution of Income and Wealth in Japan," *Review of Income and Wealth* 38, 4 (December): 403-428.

Beach, C., and G. Slottsve. 1994. "Are We Becoming Two Societies? Income Polarization and the Middle Class in Canada." Mimeo, Queens University, November.

Birdsall, N., D. Ross, and R. Sabot. 1995. "Inequality and Growth Reconsidered: Lessons from East Asia," *World Bank Economics Review* 9, 3: 477-508.

Bjorklund, A., 1992. "Rising Female Labour Force Participation and the Distribution of Family Income—The Swedish Experience," *Acta Sociologica* 35: 299-309.

Bjorklund, A., and R. Freeman. 1994. "Generating Equality and Eliminating Poverty The Swedish Way." NBER Working Paper #4945, Cambridge, December.

Brandolini, A., and P. Sestito. 1993. "La distribuzione dei redditi familiari in Italia, 1997-1991," *Servizio Studi*, Banca d'Italia.

Buhmann, B., L. Rainwater, G. Schmaus, and T. Smeeding. 1988. "Equalivance Scales, Well-Being, Inequality and Poverty: Sensitivity Estimates across Ten Countries Using the Luxembourg Income Study (LIS) Database," *Review of Income and Wealth* 34: 115-142.

Burkhauser, Richard V., Amy Crews, Mary C. Daly, and Stephen A. Jenkins. 1996. "Where in the World is the Middle Class? A Cross-National Comparison of the Shrinking Middle Class Using Kernel Density Estimates." Cross-National Studies in Aging Program Project Paper No. 26, All-University Gerontology Center, The Maxwell School, Syracuse University.

Callan, T., and B. Nolan. 1993. "Income Inequality and Poverty in Ireland in the 1970s and 1980s." ESRI Working Paper 43, Dublin.

Cantillon, B.D., I. Marx, D. Proost, and R. VanDam. 1994. "Indicateurs sociaux: 1985-1992." Centrum voor Sociaal Beleid, University of Antwerp.

Commission of the European Communities. 1993a. *Social Protection in Europe, 1993*. Brussels, Belgium: Directorate General for Employment, Industrial Relations and Social Affairs.

_____. 1993b. "Recent Reforms in Social Protection Systems in the Community." In *Social Protection in Europe, 1993*. Brussels, Belgium: Directorate General for Employment, Industrial Relations and Social Affairs.

Concialdi, P. 1995. "Income Distribution in France: The Mid-1980s Turning Point." In *The Distribution of Economic Welfare in the 1980's,* Gottschalk, Gustafsson, and Palmer, eds. Cambridge, MA: Cambridge University Press.

Deaton, A., and C. Paxson. 1994. "Intertemporal Choice and Inequality," *Journal of Political Economy* 102, 3: 437-467.

Duncan, G., T. Smeeding, and W. Rodgers. 1994. "W(h)ither the Middle Class?: A Dynamic View." In *Economic Inequality at the Close of the 20th Century,* D. Papadimitriou and E. Wolff, eds. New York: MacMillan.

Epland, J. 1992. "Innteksfordelingen i 80-årene," *Økonomiske analyser* 2: 17-26.

Erickson, C., and A.C. Ichino. 1992. "Wage Differentials in Italy: Market Forces, Institutions and Inflation." Paper presented to the National Bureau of Economic Research Conference, July.

Förster, M. 1993. "Poverty in OECD Countries," Social Policy Studies No. 10. Paris: OECD, October.

_____. 1994. "The Net Effects of Transfers on Low Incomes among Non-Elderly Families," OECD Economic Studies No. 22. Paris: OECD, Spring.

Foster, J., and M. Wolfson. 1992. "Polarization and the Decline of the Middle Class: Canada and the U.S." Mimeo, Vanderbilt University.

Freeman, R. 1994. *Working under Different Rules*. New York: Russell Sage Foundation.

Gardiner, K. 1993. "A Survey of Income Inequality over the Last Twenty Years—How Does the United Kingdom Compare?" Welfare State Programme Discussion Paper WSP/100. London School of Economics.

Goodman, A., and S. Webb. 1994. *For Richer, for Poorer*. Commentary No. 42. London: Institute for Fiscal Studies.

Gottschalk, P., and S. Danziger. 1995. *America Unequal*. New York: Russell Sage Foundation, October.

Gottschalk, P., B. Gustafsson, and E. Palmer. 1995. "What's Behind the Increase in Inequality?" Mimeo, Boston College, October.

Gottschalk, P., and T. Smeeding. 1996. "Cross-National Comparisons of Levels and Trends in Inequality." Mimeo, Boston College and Center for Advanced Study, March.

Gustafsson, B., and E.E. Palmer. 1993. "Changes in Swedish Inequality: A Study of Equivalent Income 1975-1991." University of Gothenburg.

Hagenaars, A., K. deVos, and A. Zaidi. 1994. "Patterns of Poverty in Europe." Mimeo, University of Leiden, July.

Hanratty, M., and R. Blank. 1993. "Down and Out in North America: Recent Trends in Poverty Rates in the U.S. and Canada," *Quarterly Journal of Economics* 10 (February): 223-257.

Hauser, R., and J. Becker. 1993. "The Development of the Income Distribution in the Federal Republic of Germany During the Seventies and Eighties." Mimeo, University of Frankfurt.

Jenkins, S. 1995. "Accounting for Inequality Trends in the U.K., 1971-1986," *Economica* 62 (February): 29-64.

Johnson, P., and S. Webb. 1993. "Explaining the Growth in U.K. Income Inequality," *Economic Journal* 103: 429-443.

Karoly, L. 1995. "Anatomy of U.S. Income Distribution." Rand Corporation, September.

Messere, K.C. 1994. *Tax Policy in OECD Countries: Choices and Conflicts.* Amsterdam, Netherlands: Publications BV.

Milanovic, B. 1995. "Determinants of Cross-Country Income Inequality: An Augmented Kuznets' Hypothesis." In *Income Distribution During the Transition,* Research Project Paper No. 5, The World Bank.

Muffells, F., and J. Nellison. 1995. "The Distribution of Economic Well-Being in the Netherlands, Its Evolution in the 1980s." In *Distribution of Economic Welfare in the 1980s,* Gottschalk, Gustafsson, and Palmer, eds. Cambridge, MA: University Press.

Organization for Economic Co-operation and Development (OECD). 1994. "New Orientations for Social Policy." Social Policy Studies No. 12. Paris: OECD.

Ploug, N., and J. Kvist (eds.). 1994. *Recent Trends in Cash Benefits in Europe.* Copenhagen: Danish National Institute of Social Research.

Rodrigues, C. 1993. "The Measurement and Decomposition of Inequality in Portugal, 1980/81-1989/90." Microsimulation Unit Discussion Paper 9302, Cambridge University.

Saunders, P. 1994. "Rising on the Tasman Tide: Income Inequality in Australia and New Zealand in the 1980s." SPRC Discussion Paper No. 49, University of New South Wales.

Smeeding, T., and P. Gottschalk. 1995. "The International Evidence on Income Distribution in Modern Economies: Where Do We Stand?" LIS Working Paper No. 137, December.

Smeeding, T., L. Rainwater, and M. O'Higgins. 1990. *Poverty, Inequality and the Distribution of Income in an International Context: Initial Research from the Luxembourg Income Study (LIS)*. London: Wheatsheaf Books.

Smeeding, T., L. Rainwater, and B.B. Torrey. 1993. "Going to Extremes: The U.S. Elderly in an International Context." LIS Working Paper No. 89, June.

Smeeding, T., P. Saunders, J. Coder, S. Jenkins, J. Fritzell, A. Hagenaars, R. Hauser, and M. Wolfson. 1993. "Poverty, Inequality and Family Living Standard Impacts Across Seven Nations: The Effect of Noncash Subsidies," *Review of Income and Wealth* 39 (September): 229-254.

Statistics Canada. 1994. "Income after Tax Distribution By Size." Catalogue #13-210, Ottawa.

Tachabanaki, T., and T. Yagi. 1995. "Distribution of Economic Well-Being in Japan: Towards a More Unequal Society." In *Distribution of Economic Welfare in the 1980s,* Gottschalk, Gustafsson, and Palmer, eds. Cambridge, MA: Cambridge University Press.

Torrey, B., T. Smeeding, and D. Bailey. 1996. "Rowing Between Scylla and Charybdis? Income Transitions in Central European Households." LIS Working Paper No. 132, February.

U.S. Bureau of the Census. 1995a. "Income, Poverty, and Valuations of Noncash Benefits: 1993," *Current Population Reports*, Series P-60, No. 188, February.

_____. 1995b. "Special Tabulations," courtesy of John Coder, U.S. Bureau of the Census.

Uusitalo, H. 1994. *Income Distribution in Finland*. Helsinki: Central Statistical Office of Finland.

Wolff, E. 1994. "International Comparisons of Wealth Inequality." Mimeo, New York University, September.

_____. 1995. *Top Heavy: A Study of Increasing Inequality of Wealth in America*. New York: 20th Century Fund.

From Parent to Child
Intergenerational Relations
and Intrahousehold Allocations

Jere R. Behrman
University of Pennsylvania

Perceptions are widespread that in the United States there has been increasing inequality and persistent, or perhaps increasing, poverty in recent years. The family is viewed as critical in the determination of individuals' income generation capacities, particularly through human resource investments in schooling, but also through the home environment and other channels. In this chapter, I address two sets of questions that are related to these perceptions.

First, what is the extent of intergenerational mobility? How associated across generations is income? There have long been different views on the answers to these questions. On the one hand, there are perceptions of many observers dating at least back to de Tocqueville that the United States is an open society in which mobility is relatively great, with reinforcement by the Horatio Alger stories of advancement from the mailroom to the board room and many anecdotes about "rags to riches" in one generation (and sometimes back to rags in another). On the other hand, there are allegations that often children are "chips off the old block," "biology is destiny," and "the acorn falls close to the trunk." There is an intergenerational transfer of economic status, with poor parents having poor children, while the children of the rich are born "with a silver spoon in their mouths," and according to Herrnstein and Murray in *The Bell Curve* (1994), the heritability of intelligence and perhaps other traits further limits intergenerational mobility.

Second, what is the nature of intrafamily allocations, particularly of schooling, among children? Are such allocations in response to genetic endowments? Do they tend to reinforce those endowments so that better-endowed children receive more, thus increasing earnings inequality? Or do they compensate for such endowments? If schooling allocations reinforce such endowments, do financial transfers from parents to children compensate for the earnings differentials? In making these allocations do parents weigh all children equally, or do they prefer some children identified, perhaps, by gender or birth order?

The objective of this chapter is to consider some elements of how social scientists describe and analyze phenomena related to these two sets of questions. A central point is that it is difficult to identify causality from associations in data that reflect behavioral choices made in part in response to factors that are not observed in the data by analysts. A key example is provided by child genetic endowments related to such attributes as ability, personality, persistence, and motivation. If parents make allocations of schooling in part in response to such endowments and these endowments also have direct effects on earnings, then the association between schooling and earnings does <u>not</u> reflect simply the impact of schooling on earnings, but also the effects of the unobserved endowments on earnings to the extent that they are correlated with schooling. Our grandmothers know that Mary did well in school because she was smart and diligent, and that these characteristics—in addition to schooling—served her well in the job market. Therefore, to estimate the impact of schooling per se on Mary's earnings there would have to be control for her smartness and diligence, control that simple associations do not provide.

Describing Intergenerational Associations

How strong are intergenerational associations? As noted, popular characterizations range considerably, from very low ones implied by Horatio Alger stories and other "rages to riches" fables, to very high ones implied by the "intergenerational culture of poverty" and *The Bell Curve* characterizations. Two major means of describing such associations are through correlation coefficients and through heritability estimates.

Intergenerational correlation exists when some characteristic of the parents is a determinant of that characteristic for their children. For instance, it could be that the income of a child is dependent on that of its parents. If so, a person's economic status is not entirely the product of his or her abilities and choices; those of his parents also impact on the child's income. If a positive relationship between the incomes of parents and children exists, then the children of low-income parents would, on average, be poorer than the children of high-income parents. But while such a relationship may inhibit social mobility, it does not imply a class society, or that economic status will be passed on from generation to generation.

To illustrate, suppose that the line labeled T in figure 1, the 45° line, shows the relationship between the income of parents and children, *ceteris paribus*. Then there is absolutely no social mobility. The children's income will always equal the parents' income. On the other hand, suppose the T' line indicates how a child's income changes as the income of the parents changes. In this case, though the children of high/low income parents tend to have high/low incomes, over successive generations a family's income converges to Y. In this society, there is regression toward the mean. However, this process may not be particularly rapid. For example, if Y is $40,000 and the slope of T' is 0.8, it takes eight generations for a family's income to increase from $10,000 to $34,500.

Figure 1. Parental-Child Income Positively Correlated

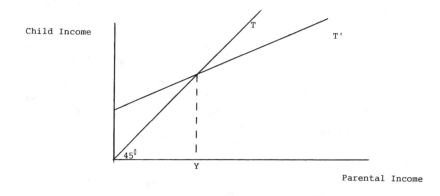

What is the evidence regarding the extent of intergenerational parent-child income correlations in the United States? There are relatively few estimates because not many data sets have information on the incomes of two generations (see estimates and surveys in Becker and

Tomes 1986 and Behrman and Taubman 1985). Until recently, the available studies were all based on one year of data. These studies indicated a correlation of about 0.2, that for every additional dollar of parental income, child income tended to increase by about 20 cents. This suggests a positive association between parental and family income, but not an overwhelming one. Such estimates suggest considerable intergenerational mobility, with many Horatio Algers and reverse Horatio Algers.

One problem with these estimates, however, is that one year of reported income data may not represent very well income over longer periods of time. There may be reporting errors as well as fluctuations in incomes from year to year because of fluctuations in the economy, the luck of individuals, or choices that people make that affect their incomes. Such fluctuations mean that estimates based on one year are likely to understate the extent of the intergenerational income associations over longer periods. It would seem then that the associations over periods longer than a year are what is of interest in describing intergenerational mobility. The question of primary interest is whether children who have relatively high-income parents during the children's childhood years are likely to have relatively high income themselves over their adult years, not for any particular year.

Recently data sets have been available in which income information on parents and on their adult children has been collected for a number of years. These data permit the exploration of the possibility that previous studies overestimated intergenerational mobility because they used only one year of income data. Estimates made from these data find that using up to ten years of income data makes a considerable difference in the estimated intergenerational correlation, and in fact, cause it to roughly double to about 0.4, with the implication that for every additional dollar of parental income child income is about 40 cents higher (Behrman and Taubman 1990; Solon 1992; Zimmermann 1992). Thus, controlling for something as simple as the fluctuations in income from year to year makes a considerable difference in the estimates of intergenerational mobility and leads to estimates of considerably less mobility and considerably stronger familial associations.

Heritability estimates indicate the proportion of the total variance in some observed outcome (phenotype) such as income that is associated with the variance in genetic endowments (genotype). Standard estimates assume that the phenotype is related to the genotype and to other determinants in a simple linear relation in which the genetic effects and the other relevant factors each can be summarized in one indicator, with no interaction between them. Such estimates are common in the literature that attempts to identify the importance of "nature" (genetic endowments) versus "nurture" (other influences on the phenotype, including behavioral choices such as schooling investments). Heritability estimates can range in value from 0 to 1, with the variance in genotype a larger share of the variance in phenotype the higher the estimate.

Heritability estimates usually are obtained from data on phenotype of twins by using the fact that identical twins have identical genetic endowments but fraternal twins have differing genetic endowments. Therefore, if genetic endowments are important, phenotypes are more similar for identical twins than for fraternal twins. For example, for the National Academy of Science-National Research Council sample of white male twins born in the United States between 1917 and 1927 who subsequently served in the military, the correlation in earnings is 0.56 for identical twins and 0.32 for fraternal twins, which implies a heritability estimate of 0.48.[1] That is, the ratio of the variation in earnings due to variations in genotypes is about half of the total variation in earnings. In *The Bell Curve*, Herrnstein and Murray (1994) claim that most measures of heritability for IQ in the United States recently tend to be in the range of 0.4 to 0.8. Estimates of these magnitudes often have been interpreted to mean that nature (genotypes) is quite important, leaving little scope for the impact of nurture through, for example, schooling. Herrnstein and Murray give such an interpretation.

But changes in nurture may have large impacts even if heritability estimates are high. Consider, for illustration, the situation in which there are only two genotypes (G_1 and G_2), each of which accounts for half of the population. Both phenotypes respond to "nurture" as in figure 2. In this figure, income is measured on the vertical axis and nurture is measured on the horizontal axis. Both genotypes respond positively to nurture, so the income lines for each of the genotypes is upward-sloping. But genotype 2 is assumed to have greater genetic endowments, so the line for this genotype is higher than for genotype 1. Assume further that half of the members of each genotype are exposed to nurture level 1 and half are exposed to nurture level 2. Therefore, one quarter of the population will have the income-genotype-nurture combinations indicated by each of the points marked a, b, c, and d. Then, as figure 2 is drawn, the heritability estimate will be high. Most of the observed variation in income is due to the difference between the two genotypes.

Figure 2. High Heritability But Still Large Impact of Changing "Nurture"

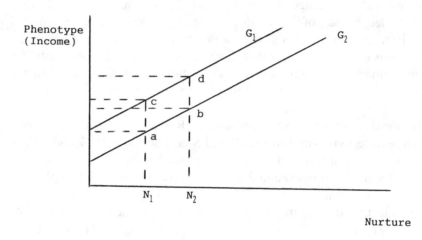

But this does *not* mean that nurture has no effect. To the contrary, increasing nurture—say, by increasing schooling—has a positive effect on income. The high value of heritability only reflects the relatively small difference between nurture levels 1 and 2. Indeed, the heritability estimate would be much smaller if the same two genotypes were divided equally between nurture levels 1 and 3 instead of between 1 and 2. The basic point is that to evaluate the impact of nurture through schools or other means, the slopes of the lines are what are of interest. This impact may be large whether the heritability estimate is large or small. The small estimate for heritability does not tell us what would happen if nurture were to be changed. But often the literature on "nature versus nurture" is not clear on this critical point. For example, Herrnstein and Murray (1994) suggest that because heritability estimates are high, schooling and other forms of nurture are not very effective. As is illustrated in figure 2, this is not a logical deduction.

What Underlies Family Allocations among Children?

The descriptions provided by correlations and heritability estimates summarized earlier are consistent with families being important in determining children's economic experiences as adults. This raises questions about how families allocate resources among children. For example, do families allocate human resources, such as schooling, in response to children's genetic endowments? Do they allocate resources so as to reinforce or to compensate for differences in genetic endowments? Do they have greater concern about some children—say, identified by sex or birth order—than others?

Economists have developed different models of intrahousehold allocations that provide a framework for thinking about such questions. Such frameworks are useful because it is difficult to analyze these (and other) behaviors that in part are in response to variables not observable by social scientists but that affect the decisions being made—in this case, genetic endowments of children. Because of such unobservable variables, one cannot simply look at associations (correlations) among observed variables in order to answer questions such as those posed above. I consider two models of intrahousehold allocations below in which parents make the decisions regarding allocations of human resources among their children.[2] Before turning to these models, however, I introduce some basic elements common to the models.

In these models, parents are assumed to maximize their satisfaction by deciding how much to invest in the schooling of each of their children. Parents are interested in their own consumption, but in order to sharpen considerations about how they allocate resources among their children, I assume that the allocation of resources among the children is separable from the parents' decision about how they themselves consume. I also assume that the parents' satisfaction increases as any child's income rises, *ceteris paribus*.

As in any economic model of household choice, the incomes that parents "choose" for their children depend on the exact nature of parental preferences and a budget constraint—in this case, the income possibilities frontier, those combinations of incomes that are attainable by the children. The income possibilities frontier would presumably have the appearance of the textbook production possibilities frontier; its precise curvature and position would depend on the endowments of each child, the resources that the parents devote to their children, the prices of schooling, and so forth.

Figure 3 shows how the parents' preferences and the income possibilities frontier interact to determine each child's income. Two characteristics of equal-satisfaction curves are of interest. First, there is the "distribution-total income" tradeoff, which relates to the curvature of the equal-satisfaction curves. If equal-satisfaction curves are straight lines, parents are only concerned with the total income of their children. The distribution of this income among the children is unimportant to the parents. In contrast, if these curves are rectangular (L-shaped), parental satisfaction increases only if the incomes of both children increase. In this case, the primary concern is with how income is distributed between children. If these curves have the textbook curvature of indifference curves, both total income and its distribution are of concern to parents.

Figure 3. Constrained Maximization of Parental Satisfaction Regarding Child Income

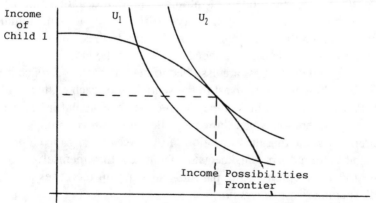

A second characteristic of these curves that merits attention is their symmetry, or lack thereof. These curves are symmetric if switching the incomes of two children has no effect on the satisfaction of their parents. If equal-satisfaction curves do not have this property, parents care which child receives the higher income when some total income is distributed between the two children. If equal-satisfaction curves are symmetric and children have equal endowments, parents will invest in the education of their children and make financial transfer so as to produce equal incomes for their children. However, if either of these conditions do not hold, income equality will not necessarily obtain.

Currently, the wealth model (Becker and Tomes 1976) is the paradigm that economists most commonly use to analyze intrafamily allocation of resources. In the wealth model, parents are concerned only with the total wealth of each child, not with its composition of sources. Therefore, they do not distinguish between earned income and unearned income. If parents both invest in the schooling of their children and transfer financial and physical assets to their children, they do so in order to maximize the total wealth of the children. This of course requires that parents increase their investment in the education of a child as long as the marginal rate of return to that investment exceeds the rate of return on financial assets.

In the wealth model, as originally presented by Becker and Tomes, it is assumed that parents provide enough resources to their children that all children receive financial transfers in addition to wealth-maximizing investments in schooling. Parents invest in the human capital of each child until the marginal rate of return to education is driven down to the rate of return on financial assets; any additional resources provided to children take the form of transfers such as gifts and bequests. Parents with more than one child and equal concern for all their children (symmetric equal-satisfaction curves) use transfers to offset fully inequalities in their children's earnings. Hence, the wealth model with equal concern predicts a pattern of unequal earnings, unequal transfers, and equal wealth. But parents' investments in their children's human capital are socially efficient provided there are no externalities and well-functioning capital markets.

However, the assumption that parents are rich enough and altruistic enough that they provide all of their children the wealth-maximizing level of schooling is critical (Behrman, Pollak, and Taubman 1995). If parents do not allocate "enough" resources to their children, then some children receive less than the socially efficient level of human capital, and those children receive zero transfer. In this case, (a) schooling investments are not efficient, and (b) even if parents have equal concern, the incomes of the children are not equalized because the child with greater endowments receives greater schooling investments and earns greater income, but transfers are not used to equalize total income between the children.

In contrast to Becker and Tomes, the separable earnings transfer (SET) model of Behrman, Pollak, and Taubman (1982) assumes that parents care differently about income that their children earn from working than about income their children receive from clipping bond coupons. So, they consider the distribution of earnings among their children separately from the distribution of nonearnings income.

The SET model has two important different implications from those of the wealth model with substantial resources devoted to children as originally presented by Becker and Tomes. First, the SET model does not imply that human capital investments are efficient, even with well-functioning capital markets and no externalities. If parents value earnings income more than nonearnings income, for example, they may invest more in the schooling of a child than wealth-maximizing. Second, it does not imply that parents with equal concern for their children attempt to offset fully differences in earnings by allocating transfers unequally. The consideration of earnings separately from transfers in fact means that there is no relation between earnings gaps between siblings and patterns of transfers received from parents. Therefore, rather than equal income among children in the same family with different endowments, the SET model generally implies unequal income. While these are important differences in comparison with the Becker and Tomes original formulation of the wealth model, the wealth model implications when parents do not devote enough resources to their children to provide positive transfers to each are similar (though not identical since the SET model results are consistent with positive transfers).

Data limitations make it difficult to estimate critical parameters of either of these models directly or to distinguish empirically between the wealth model and the SET model. Some critical variables simply are not observable in any data set, namely endowments and marginal rates of return to schooling for individuals. Other data are only partially observed. For example, to assess these models it would be desirable to have lifetime transfers (inter vivos and bequests) received by all children in a family from their parents and lifetime schooling investments and earnings. But at best data sets provide a subset of this information. Nevertheless, by using special data on adult siblings and in some cases specific assumptions about the underlying relations, some progress has been made in estimating critical dimensions of these intrahousehold allocation models. I discuss three examples.

First, conditional on particular functional forms for parental levels of satisfaction and for the impact of genetic endowments and schooling on earnings, estimates of the SET model provide insight into the total income-distribution tradeoff and unequal concern in the parental objective function underlying intrahousehold allocations (Behrman, Pollak and Taubman 1982, 1986; Behrman and Taubman 1986; Behrman 1988a, 1988b). For the United States, these estimates indicate that investments in schooling are not determined solely by concerns about maximizing total income of the children: distribution also weighs heavily in intrafamily allocations. For rural India, a much poorer society, similar results have been found for the allocation of nutrients among children during the surplus season when food is relatively abundant, but during the lean season when food is scarce, allocation is determined almost entirely by productivity concerns.

Parents might provide unequal education to daughters and sons because their preferences favor children of one gender or because they know that the labor market rewards unequally women and men with the same ability and the same human capital. Estimates of the SET model show that the preferences of parents in the United States do not favor sons over daughters; indeed, if marriage market as well as labor market returns are incorporated into the analysis, the empirical evidence suggests that parents' preferences give slightly more weight to daughters than to sons. These results contrast with the finding that there is unequal concern favoring sons in the lean season in rural India.

Birth-order effects have been widely discussed in the biological, psychological, and popular literatures. Lower birth-order children (i.e., older children) may benefit from developing in more adult-oriented environments and from teaching their younger siblings. Higher birth-order children, on the other hand, may benefit from having more experienced parents. Casual observation (perhaps primarily by older siblings) suggests that the youngest child is often spoiled by excessive parental attention and indulgence. Finally, birth order may be related to health because of the relationship between birth order and mother's age, with less healthy children borne by very young and very old mothers.

Birth order may affect intrafamily allocation through preferences or through constraints. On the preference side, parents may fail to exhibit equal concern and instead favor the eldest or youngest child. On the constraint side, parents with many children may allocate less to each child, and borrowing constraints may vary over the parents' life cycle, differentially affecting children of different birth orders. Estimates of the SET model find that intrafamily allocations favor children of lower birth order both for the United States and for rural Indian in the lean season. For the United States, borrowing constraints are part of the explanation.

Second, an implication of the wealth model with high resources given to children and equal concern is that differences in income yielded by transfers of financial and physical assets given to children offset differences in labor market earnings of children in the same family. The data, however, show that for most households the absolute magnitudes of gifts and bequests are insufficient to offset fully earnings differentials among siblings (Behrman, Pollak, and Taubman 1995; Menchik 1979, 1980, 1988; Wilhelm 1991). Moreover, the dominant pattern for bequests—equal or almost equal bequests for all children in the same family—is not consistent with bequests offsetting earnings differentials among children in the same family. Differences in inter vivos transfers to children do compensate a little for differences in their earnings, but offset very little of these differences. Finally, for families for which the resources devoted to children are not sufficient that all children receive transfers, the wealth model still implies that one child may receive transfers. But available data on bequests indicates that it is rare that one but only one child receives bequests. Thus, all in all, the data on transfers to children, though fragmentary, does not provide much support for the wealth model. They are consistent, however, with the SET model.

Third, there are recent estimates, based on minimal assumptions, of whether intrahousehold allocations of schooling investments are in response to endowments and, if so, whether they reinforce endowment differentials or compensate for endowment differentials among siblings. These estimates utilize data on adult identical and, in some cases, fraternal twins.[3] The essence of the procedures used to obtain these estimates is now illustrated with reference to the following relations.

Assume that earnings of the ith child (E_1) in a family depends linearly on that child's schooling (S_1), an unobserved family earnings endowment that is common to all children in the family (f), an unobserved child-specific endowment that distinguishes that child from the common family endowment (a_1), and a random error term (e_1) due to measurement error in earnings. Then for two children in a family, the earnings relations are:[4]

(1) $E_1 = b S_1 + f + a_1 + e_i$

and

(2) $E_2 = b S_2 + f + a_2 + e_2$

where b is the true impact of schooling. Assume further that there are linear schooling allocation rules that indicate how parents allocate schooling to two children depending on the unobserved endowments of each (a_1, a_2), some common family characteristics including parental wealth and education and the common family endowments (X), and random disturbance terms (u_1 and u_2, respectively):

(3) $S_1 = \alpha_1 a_1 + \alpha_2 a_2 + \beta X + u_1$

and

(4) $S_2 = \alpha_1 a_2 + \alpha_2 a_1 + \beta X + u_2$

where α_1 is the parental schooling allocation response to the endowment of the child being invested in α_2 is the parental schooling allocation response to the endowment of the other child, and β is the parental schooling allocation response common family characteristics. If a_1 is positive and α_2 is negative, parents reinforce endowment differentials by investing more in the schooling of the child with greater endowments, thus increasing the inequality of the distribution of earnings. If

α_1 is negative and α_2 is positive, parents compensate for endowment differentials by investing more in the schooling of the child with lesser endowments, thus reducing inequality in the distribution of earnings.

The critical parameters in neither the earnings relations nor the schooling allocation relations can be estimated consistently with data on individuals or even on siblings. To see why, consider what happens if one tries to estimate the schooling effect on earnings (i.e., the parameter b) from relation (1) and observations on schooling and earnings for a number of individuals. The problem is that the schooling allocation rule in relation (3) means that schooling is correlated with family (f, which is in X) and individual-specific endowments (a_1). Those who are more schooled are likely to have greater endowments, so the usual procedure of simply associating individual earnings with individual schooling does *not* indicate the effect of schooling alone on earnings.

Figure 4 illustrates this problem. The solid line gives the true relation between earnings and schooling, with a slope b. For individuals, however, data observations in general are not on this true line because of the random disturbance term (e_1) and because of the unobserved endowments ($f + a_1$). The random disturbance term takes on values that are independent of schooling, so it does not cause the estimated slope of the line to shift. However, if those with more ability tend to have more schooling, the unobserved endowments are likely to be larger for those with more schooling. Figure 4 illustrates the impact of endowments that deviate positively from the average at high schooling levels and negatively from the average at low schooling levels (with γ reflecting the relation of the unobserved endowments with schooling) and how they twist the estimated earnings-schooling relation if they are not controlled in the estimation. If there is not control for such unobserved endowments, what is estimated by looking at the association between earnings and schooling is not the slope of the true relation, but the slope of the dashed line, which reflects in part the effects of the endowments in addition to the effects of schooling. Thus, the usual procedure of associating schooling with earnings without control for endowments might overstate substantially the impact of schooling on earnings and other outcomes.

**Figure 4. True and Estimated Impact of Schooling on Earnings If
Schooling Allocated in Response to Endowments**

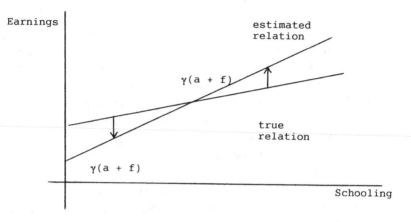

How might endowments be controlled in order to obtain better estimates of the impact of schooling on earnings? One possibility would be to follow the lead of the experimental sciences and randomly assign schooling rather than letting families decide on schooling. This would eliminate the estimation problem caused by schooling being allocated in response to endowments, but in most societies would be very difficult to do. A second possibility is to control for endowments using proxies such as IQ test scores. If endowments can be controlled completely through such observed measures, a consistent estimate of the true schooling effects can be obtained. But it is not clear that it is possible to measure all aspects of endowments. Moreover, some of the observed indicators that have been proposed to be used to control for endowments, such as IQ scores, may represent not only endowments but also dimensions of behavior including treatment at home and schooling.

A third possibility is to use data on identical twins to estimate the difference between relations (1) and (2):

(5) $E_1 - E_2 = b(S_1 - S_2) + (f - F) + (a_1 - a_2) + (e_1 - e_2)$.

The effects of the family components of endowments disappear in such a relation. For identical twins (and only for identical twins) there are only common endowments (not individual-specific endowments), so estimation of relation (5) eliminates biases due to endowments.[5] Early estimates using this procedure indicate that the true impact of schooling on earnings is only about a third as large suggested by associations that do not control for endowments (Behrman and Taubman 1976; Behrman, Hrubec, Taubman, and Wales 1980).

But this procedure exacerbates another possible estimation problem noted earlier with regard to intergenerational correlations: measurement error. Random measurement error in a right-side variable in a relation such as (1) causes the coefficient estimate of that variable to be biased toward zero. If the schooling measure used is noisy due to measurement error, in other words, the true impact of schooling on earnings is partially disguised and underestimated. Differencing between two schooling measures as in relation (5) if each is contaminated by noise exacerbates the bias towards zero due to measurement error. A series of recent studies has applied the twins estimator in relation (5) with control for measurement error (Ashenfelter and Krueger 1994; Behrman, Rosenzweig and Taubman 1994, 1996). These studies all find that control for measurement error reduces the apparent biases in the standard studies due to failure to control for unobserved endowments. But for four of the five twins samples used, the estimates still indicate that there are significant upward biases in the standard estimates of the impact of schooling on earnings because of the failure to control for endowments. For some of the U.S. samples, moreover, the proportion of the variance in earnings due to such endowments is considerable: 27 percent of the total for men and 7 percent of the total for women due in individual-specific endowment variations within families (plus another 16 percent for women due to variability in family endowments) in the studies in Behrman, Rosenzweig and Taubman (1994, 1996).

Most of these studies, thus, imply that intrahousehold allocations of schooling are in response to endowments. But estimation of relation (5) alone with identical twins cannot indicate whether, if endowments differ among children, such allocations reinforce or compensate for such differences. Two of these recent twins studies (Behrman, Rosenzweig and Taubman 1994, 1996), however, develop a procedure for estimating whether there is reinforcement or compensation in the schooling allocation rules by using both identical and fraternal twins and by estimating together with relation (5) the difference in the school allocations rules (obtained by subtracting relation (4) from relation (3):

(6) $S_1 - S_2 = (\alpha_1 - \alpha_2)(a_1 - a_2) + (u_1 - u_2)$.

Intuitively, their procedure is equivalent to obtaining a consistent estimate of the parameter b from estimating relation (5) with identical twins, using this parameter to obtain an estimate of $(a_1 - a_2)$ by estimating relation (5) for fraternal twins, and then using this estimate of $(a_1 - a_2)$ to estimate relation (6) for fraternal twins and thus obtain an estimate of $(\alpha_1 - \alpha_2)$. If the estimate of $(\alpha_1 - \alpha_2)$ is positive, parents invest in schooling of their children so as to reinforce endowment differentials and increase income inequalities (and vice versa if $(\alpha_1 - \alpha_2)$ is negative). The estimates indicate that there is parental reinforcement in that children with greater endowments have greater schooling and more resource-intensive (higher quality) schooling. For men, for example, these estimates imply that positive reinforcement of endowments by intrahousehold allocations increases by about 80 percent absolute earnings differentials that emanate from preschool individual-specific endowment differentials.

Conclusions

Family background may play an important role in determining the distribution of income and who is rich and who is poor. Estimates of intergenerational correlations and of heritability are consistent with a major role of family background in determining individuals' economic success. With control for measurement error in earnings, the U.S. intergenerational experience seems characterized by many more individuals born into a "culture of poverty" or "with a silver spoon in their mouths" than by Horatio Alger "rags to riches" (or reverse Horatio Alger "riches to rags") stories. But it is important to remember that correlation or heritability descriptions of limited intergenerational mobility in themselves do not provide direct information about the effectiveness of schooling and other means for affecting economic outcomes. Though this point is often misunderstood, even if heritability estimates are high, schooling and other measures may be quite effective in altering economic outcomes.

The high association for economic outcomes across generations, nevertheless, suggests that what happens within households may have important implications for children's economic alternatives. Models have been developed of intrahousehold allocations of schooling and other human resource investments among children in the presence of unobserved (by social scientists but observed by the parents) heterogenous endowments of the children. The predominant model of intrahousehold allocations, the wealth model, suggests that parents with equal concern who allocate enough resources to their children will (a) invest in the schooling of their children at socially efficient levels if there are not market imperfections, and (b) provide transfers of assets the income from which will offset earnings differentials among their children. An alternative, the Separable Earnings Transfer (SET) model, (a) suggests that even with no market imperfections parents will not necessarily invest in the schooling of their children at socially optimal levels, and (b) posits that the pattern of earnings among these children (resulting from their endowments and schooling) is not related to the pattern of parental resource transfers among these children.

Empirical exploration of these intrahousehold models and their implications is difficult because of data limitations both regarding child endowments and regarding the lifetime economic interactions between children and their parents. But progress has been made with special data, such as data on adult siblings including twins, their economic status, and their economic interactions with their parents. Empirical explorations to date suggest some tentative conclusions. Transfers to children do not compensate for earnings differentials as posited in the wealth model with equal concern and sufficient parental resources devoted to children, so earnings differentials induced by intrahousehold allocations among children of schooling carry over to total income differentials. Parental allocations of human resources among their children in the United States tend to reflect some concern about distribution among the children rather than just maximizing total income of the children, with some unequal concern favoring those of lower birth order (though not according to gender). In contrast, in the much poorer society of rural India, there is much less concern about distribution and there is unequal concern favoring sons when resources are tightest (as well as unequal concern favoring low birth order children). But still, in the United States, parents on net reinforce endowment differentials by investing more in the schooling of better-endowed children in a manner that almost doubles the impact of within-family endowment differentials on earnings. Thus, endowment differentials among children in the same families and intrahousehold allocations in response to such endowments play an important role in increasing earnings and income inequalities in the United States; the within-family endowment differentials alone account for a quarter of the variation of ln earnings for males, which is reinforced by schooling allocations to account for over two-fifths of the total variation in earnings. The importance of unobserved endowments in intrahousehold allocations, finally, reinforces the importance of considering what determines schooling in attempts to evaluate the impact of schooling on economic and other outcomes in order to attain estimates of the effects of schooling per se that are not contaminated by effects of unobserved abilities, motivations, and family connections.

NOTES

The author has benefited in preparing this paper from collaborative work with a number of individuals through the years, but particularly from work with Robert A. Pollak, Mark R. Rosenzweig, and Paul Taubman. The author also thanks Jon R. Neill and two reviewers from the Upjohn Institute for editorial suggestions that have improved the presentation.

1. It can be shown that heritability as defined above is equal to twice the difference in the correlation for identical versus fraternal twins.

2. In these two models, parents make the active decision and the children are passive. In other models, the children may attempt to actively manipulate the outcomes to their advantage (e.g., Bernheim, Shleifer, and Summers 1985; Pollak 1988). Parents also may have unified objectives or may bargain over various allocations (see survey in Behrman 1995). For simplicity, I limit my attention here to models with passive children and with parents who have unified objectives.

3. Some might question whether families with twins are so different from other families that one cannot learn much of general value from studying families with twins. But the procedures that are used to study within-family allocations to twins effectively control for the family effects (f and X below) that might reflect differences in families that have twins from other families

4. I limit this presentation to the two-child family for simplicity, but the basic points hold if there are more children in the family.

5. For any siblings, not just identical twins, the common family component is controlled with such estimates. It might appear that it is better to control for that common component with sibling data than to use individual data. But that is not necessarily true. The bias may be greater with sibling estimates due to the difference in individual-specific endowments than in individual estimates (Griliches 1979).

References

Ashenfelter, Orley, and Alan Krueger. 1994. "Estimates of the Economic Return to Schooling from a New Sample of Twins," *American Economic Review* 84, 5 (December): 1157-1174.

Becker, Gary S. 1967. "Human Capital and the Personal Distribution of Income: An Analytical Approach." Ann Arbor: University of Michigan, Woytinsky Lecture, (reprinted in Gary S. Becker, *Human Capital*, Second Edition, Columbia University Press, 1975).

_____. 1991, *A Treatise on the Family*, Cambridge, MA: Harvard University Press.

Becker, Gary S., and Nigel Tomes. 1976. "Child Endowments and the Quantity and Quality of Children," *Journal of Political Economy* 84, 4, Part 2 (August): S143-S162.

_____. 1979. "An Equilibrium Theory of the Distribution of Incomes and Intergenerational Mobility," *Journal of Political Economy* 87, 6 (December): 1153-1189.

Becker, Gary S., and Nigel Tomes. 1986. "Human Capital and the Rise and Fall of Families," *Journal of Labor Economics* 4, 3, Part II (July): S1-S39.

Behrman, Jere R. 1988a. "Intrahousehold Allocation of Nutrients in Rural India: Are Boys Favored? Do Parents Exhibit Inequality Aversion?" *Oxford Economic Papers* 40, 1 (March): 32-54.

_____. 1988b. "Nutrition, Health, Birth Order, and Seasonality: Intrahousehold Allocation in Rural India," *Journal of Development Economics* 28, 7 (February): 43-63.

_____. 1996. "Intrahousehold Distribution and the Family." In *Handbook of Population and Family Economics*, Mark R. Rosenzweig and Oded Stark, eds. Amsterdam: North-Holland.

Behrman, Jere R., Z. Hrubec, Paul Taubman, and Terence J. Wales. 1980. *Socioeconomic Success: A Study of the Effects of Genetic Endowments, Family Environment and Schooling*. Amsterdam: North-Holland.

Behrman, Jere R., Robert A. Pollak, and Paul Taubman. 1982. "Parental Preferences and Provision for Progeny," *Journal of Political Economy* 90, 1 (February): 52-73.

_____. 1986. "Do Parents Favor Boys?" *International Economic Review* 27, 1 (February): 31-52.

_____. 1995. "The Wealth Model: Efficiency in Education and Equity in the Family," In *From Parent to Child: Intrahousehold Allocations and Intergenerational Relations in the United States*, Jere R. Behrman, Robert A. Pollak, and Paul Taubman, eds. Chicago, IL: University of Chicago Press.

Behrman, Jere R., Mark R. Rosenzweig, and Paul Taubman. 1994. "Endowments and the Allocation of Schooling in the Family and in the Marriage Market: The Twins Experiment," *Journal of Political Economy* 102, 6 (December)" 1131-1174.

_____. 1996. "College Choice and Wages: Estimates Using Data on Female Twins," *Review of Economics and Statistics* 78, 4 (November): 672-685.

Behrman, Jere R., and Paul Taubman. 1976. "Intergenerational Transmission of Income and Wealth," *American Economic Review* 66, 3 (May): 436:440.

_____. 1985. "Intergenerational Earnings Mobility in the U.S.: Some Estimates and a Test of Becker's Intergenerational Endowments Model," *Review of Economics and Statistics* 67, 1 (February): 144-151.

_____. 1986. "Birth Order, Schooling, and Earnings," *Journal of Labor Economics* 4, 3 (July): S121-S145.

_____. 1989. "Is Schooling 'Mostly in the Genes'? Nature-Nurture Decomposition with Data on Relatives," *Journal of Political Economy* 97, 6 (December): 1425-1446.

_____. 1990. "Intergenerational Correlation between Children's Adult Earnings and Their Parents' Income: Results from the Michigan Panel Survey of Income Dynamics," *The Review of Income and Wealth* 36, 2 (June): 115-127.

Bernheim, B. Douglas, Andrei Shleifer, and Lawrence H. Summers. 1985. "The Strategic Bequest Motive," *Journal of Political Economy* 93, 6 (December): 1045-1076.

Griliches, Zvi. 1979. "Sibling Models and Data in Economics: Beginnings of a Survey," *Journal of Political Economy* 87, 5, Part 2 (October): S37-S64.

Herrnstein, Richard J., and Charles Murray. 1994. *The Bell Curve: Intelligence and Class Structure in American Life*. New York: Free Press.

Menchik, Paul. 1979. "Intergenerational Transmission of Inequality: An Empirical Study of Wealth Mobility," *Economica*, 46, 184 (November): 349-362.

_____. 1980. "Primogeniture, Equal Sharing and the U.S. Distribution of Wealth," *Quarterly Journal of Economics* 94, 2 (March): 299-316.

_____. 1988. "Unequal Estate Division: Is It Altruism, Reverse Bequest or Simply Noise?" In *Modelling the Accumulation and Distribution of Wealth*, Denis Kessler and Andre Masson, eds. Oxford: Oxford University Press.

Pollak, Robert A. 1988. "Tied Transfers and Paternalistic Preferences," *American Economic Review* 78, 2 (May): 240-244.

Solon, Gary. 1989. "Biases in the Estimation of Intergenerational Earnings Correlations," *Review of Economics and Statistics* 71, 1 (February): 172-174.

_____. 1992. "Intergenerational Income Mobility in the United States," *American Economic Review* 82, 3 (June): 393-408.

Wilhelm, Mark O. 1991. "Bequests Behavior and the Effect of Heir's Earnings: Testing the Altruistic Model of Bequests." Mimeo, Pennsylvania State University.

Zimmerman, David J. 1992. "Regression Toward Mediocrity in Economic Stature," *American Economic Review* 82, 3 (June): 409-429.

The Reality of Redistribution

Gordon Tullock
University of Arizona

This discussion is rather unusual in that I cannot remember the rather simple point made in it ever having appeared in the literature. This may indicate that I have been careless in my reading, so I hope that any of you who have seen it before will let me know.

That there is a tradeoff between redistribution of income and the total production of society and its rate of growth is believed by everyone, although there is little empirical evidence. Okun actually wrote a full book on this subject, coining the phrase: "the leaky bucket." One aspect of the tradeoff, however, seems to have been ignored. I shall begin my discussion of this point with a little example using numbers that I have simply drawn out of the air.

The reader will quickly realize that the importance of the phenomenon depends very heavily on these numbers. Thus, this example is intended as illustrative only. After I have presented the example, we will turn to discussing what effect different numbers would have, consider social mobility, and deal with risk aversion. This part of the chapter is, at least subjectively, original. In order to deal with some likely objections, at the end I will repeat some arguments I have used before on relative deprivation and international transfers, and then turn to a few remarks on charitable motivation.

Redistribution and Growth

Let us assume, then, that the United States government takes measures to supplement the income of the bottom 20 percent by an average of 50 percent, funding the transfer by an income tax on the upper 80 percent. Let us assume it does this in some reasonably efficient way without going into details. This should slow down the rate of growth at least somewhat, and for purposes of this example I will assume the rate of growth falls from 5 percent a year to 3 percent.

As a result of this, the local GNP 15 years in the future will be enough smaller than it would have been had we not retarded growth by this scheme that the people in the bottom one-fifth of the population will receive lower incomes than they would have received had the transfer not been made.[1] Further, they will continue to receive lower incomes throughout all eternity with the differences steadily getting greater. The upper 80 percent were worse off from the word go unless they received enough satisfaction from helping the poor to compensate. In any event, they will be worse off even with the strong charitable motives after 15 years.

Figure 1 shows that situation. The line UU and the line LL are the income of the upper 80 percent, and the lower 20 percent without transfers. The line UP and the line LP are the post-transfer lines. The lines cross at 15 years for the poor, and UP is everywhere below UU for the well-off. The reality illustrated in this figure raises at least three questions, two regarding the purpose of the transfer scheme, the third a deep ethical question that economists tend to ignore.

The first question that we need to ask is whether this transfer has benefited the poor. Certainly this would depend upon a number of things, but most important the age of the poor person, his or her discount rate, and the effect of the transfer on the growth rate of his or her income. *Ceteris paribus*, young people would tend to regard the tradeoff as decidedly negative while poor people who happen to be the same age as the current ruler of China, Deng Hsiao-Ping, would think it a bargain. If poverty is primarily an affliction of the young and old, we have the house that redistribution is intended to benefit much divided. The public choice implications of this situation should be obvious.

The second question that comes to my mind relates to the intergenerational transfer resulting from any policy that reduces the growth rate. To look at it from the standpoint of all poor people (or the charitable well-off), the scheme would mean that in the future all poor people are poorer than they otherwise would be. On the other hand, with the economy growing anyway, people who are made poorer, i.e., the poor in the future, would nevertheless be better off than the people who are poor right now. Thus, it could be regarded as a transfer from the future population—rich, poor, and middle-class—to the bottom 20 percent now.[2]

Figure 1. Income through Time

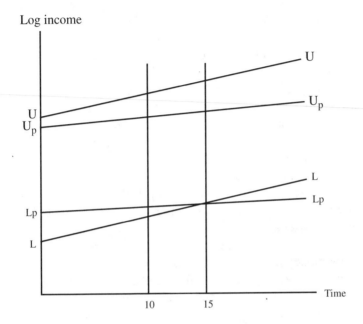

It is not obvious that this is undesirable. It is similar to the situation in which we deliberately retard investment now in order to raise current consumption with the full knowledge that the consumption in the future will be lowered, but will still be higher than it is now. However, this thinking seems only to be pertinent to affluent societies, since it is the reverse of the position taken by most development economists. What we frequently find in this literature is the recommendation that people should be compelled to increase their savings because the reduction in present consumption would be more than paid for by the increase in future consumption.[3]

This effect can be shown on the same diagram as we have given above. All that is necessary is to assume that the UP and the LP lines are the status quo with which we start before the transfer. The government then takes money from the poor and gives it to the well-off, thus generating PP and the UU lines. This would effectively involve a tax on the poor.[4] Of course, the development economists never actually proposed this kind of thing. They were simply going to put a general tax on the present generation and use it to subsidize capital accumulation, including human capital accumulation. Their idea was to cause higher growth. They normally talked about helping the poor, but as a matter of fact, most of the taxes were drawn from the poorest of the poor, the farmers, and the principal beneficiaries were civil servants and other government associates who are far from poor.

In any event, these programs have not worked but the basic reason is not that there was anything wrong with the theory. It was that actual implementation was very badly done. The famous bridge over the lower Congo connecting one dirt track with another dirt track is only one of many examples.[5]

Most economists would agree that this program of taking funds from the poor and giving them to the well-off would accelerate growth, and you will note that all of the arguments we have made before are reversed here. After a short period of time the poor would be better off. In this case, since the poor are better off in the future rather than now, transferring money from the present day poor who are very poor to the future poor who, although poor by the standards of the future, are better off, enhances the regressive-nature of the income transfer.

Some Ethical Questions

Redistributionists seem to think that they occupy the moral high ground. As I have said on other occasions, I am puzzled by the habit of discussing redistribution within a narrow geographical context. In most discussions of income redistribution, the really poor people in the world—people who live in places like Africa, India, and China—are left out. The homeless in Tucson are bad-off by American standards, but by the standards of India, they are rather well-off. They are certainly vastly better-off than the street people of Calcutta or the street children of Columbia. They are also in many dimensions better-off than their own ancestors were a few generations back. Their medical attention in particular is better than anything available until very recently.

In any event, the decision to lower the rate of growth in the United States by making income transfers will reduce the rate of growth in other countries. We are connected to them by international trade and, perhaps more important, by the trade in ideas, particularly the ideas for new or improved devices. When the production of these falls off, living standards will fall or perhaps simply not grow as rapidly in the rest of the world. This nexus can only make the rightness of redistribution more ambiguous.

The tendency of redistributionists to be much more concerned for the people of their own nation is an interesting phenomenon. Tucson is only 100 miles from the Mexican border, and a great deal of money is spent by the federal, state, and local governments in helping the poor in Tucson, most of whom even without that help would be better off than the average Mexican. All of them would be better off than the most impoverished Mexicans. To repeat, I find this curious, but most people I talk to find it quite natural. Presumably redistributionists have a willingness to trade off their personal welfare for that of others, and like all rational agents, are less interested in this tradeoff as its cost rises. That this preference should be given moral connotation is interesting, particularly if these preferences are dependent on the ethnic identity of the parties.

In any case, there are other ethical questions that redistribution raises. Let us return to our basic discussion of the transfer of funds from upper income to the lower. I do not think that in the real world a formal program with the announced objective of taking money from the poor to benefit the upper income as a way of getting faster growth will ever be adopted.

Turning to my example, it is not clear that the transfer is to the benefit of the people at the bottom. But, as the reader will no doubt have already noticed, it depends to a considerable extent on the exact numbers that I have chosen. Suppose that the effect on growth were less. As far as I know we have no clear-cut measures of the degree to which transfers reduce growth. Suppose for example, it would be not 15 but 150 years before the incomes of the bottom 20 percent would be as low or lower than they would be without the transfer.

The first thing to be said about this is that the out-of-pocket costs to the upper 80 percent would be exactly the same in the two different examples, and transfers of this sort are normally urged in terms of the desirability of the upper class sacrificing for the lower.

Members of the lower class could all assume that they would be dead by the time the change occurred, and so they and other poor people would remain better off, indeed the children of the poor people, if they remained in the poorer class, would be better off. It would be the grandchildren and great grandchildren that would begin to suffer if families remained firmly fixed in poverty.

If we follow Barro and assume that people regarded their descendants as important as themselves, then the period of crossover would be irrelevant. The poor person would worry about his or her descendants in the year 3000 and would be opposed to the transfer. As far as I know no one except Barro actually believes that people behave that way. But if people do not, then on what moral authority do we transfer income from these future generations? Unlike the present generation of the wealthy, they have no democratic voice. They are entirely without representation, even though the burden of redistribution falls on them as surely as it falls on the present generation of wealthy citizens.

There are various numbers that would lead to the crossover point being somewhere between 15 and 150 and would lead to different attitudes on the part of the present poor. With present data we cannot say exactly how long the period would be. It seems to me that this provides an incentive for getting better numbers.

Social Mobility, Relative Deprivation, and Other Conundra

We now turn to social mobility and subsequently to aversion. I have implicitly assumed that people who are at the bottom 20 percent or in the top 80 percent will stay there, and that they expect their children to do likewise.[6] This is not true in most societies, and certainly not in ours. The poor, in particular, tend to think that their children will do better in life than they themselves have done.

Circulation is to be expected, and we have an interesting asymmetry in the effects of this scheme. For the sake of illustration, assume that the average person in the bottom 20 percent believes that he will get out of it into the top 80 percent in 10 years. He will receive transfers only for the first 10 years of the program. However, if the bottom 20 percent moves up, one quarter of the top 80 percent must move down.

For people presently in the bottom 20 percent, the expected benefit from the transfer is therefore reduced. On the other hand, the possibility of falling into the bottom 20 percent of the income distribution lessens the injury that the transfer inflicts on upper income people. Whether or not social mobility makes transfers more likely from a public choice perspective would depend on many factors.

Of course, the assumption of the change occurring at the end of 10 years is arbitrary, and also the assumption that the entire bottom group goes up. If we wanted to make a more precise argument here we would need a little algebra, but in the absence of any numbers to put in equations it doesn't seem worthwhile elaborating it. The general principles for these simple numerical examples would continue to apply.

This brings us to the topic of risk aversion. The reader, we hope, will remember that risk aversion, and the justification for income redistribution from upper income people to lower based on it was the major theme of chapter 13 in *The Calculus of Consent*.[7] Since most people buy insurance at actuarially unfair prices, there is good reason to believe that most people are risk averse. Therefore, some kind of income insurance would be attractive to most people.

With risk aversion, even if everything we have said so far were true, we might get unanimous consent for an income redistribution scheme. It presumably would not be the kind of income redistribution we see in the United States, and other advanced countries in which you don't get help just because you are poor, but only if you are in certain appropriate categories. The bureaucratic difficulties, which mean you frequently don't get help at all until sometime after its need has become acute, would also be removed.

The first question is how much people are willing to pay for such insurance. The retarding of the growth rate of the income of the poor obviously makes it more expensive than in most traditional discussions. However, a lot of this would depend on where you made your decision. You might make decisions today in favor of redistributing to the poor which 200 years from now your descendants will bitterly regret. It would be true even of poor descendants.

There is a metaphysical problem. Since risk is something that most people avoid, reducing the risk is a positive service for society. Unfortunately, it is not included in GNP, but for calculations such as we are making here we should at least mention the fact. It might be that the reduced growth rate shown in the figure is actually the growth with the service of risk reduction left out. It is not impossible, although I think it is unlikely, that the service of risk reduction, if included, could more than compensate for all the problems we have raised so far.

So far, I have merely discussed in a very vague way this particular problem. I think it would be thought of more, but it may be that it already has been thought of and carefully discussed in literature that I have not seen. To repeat, I hope any reader who knows of such litera- ture will let me know. We will now turn to material that I know has been published before but that is needed to make this chapter even rea- sonably complete.

Let us turn now to relative deprivation, and here I will be repeating arguments I have made before.[8] It is sometimes said that people are not interested particularly in their actual income but in their comparative income. An American living in Harlem is bothered more by the absence of a colored television which all the neighbors have than is a mother living in the Sahel when her child dies in a famine that takes the lives of many other children in her village.

You can see from my example that I regard it as basically an absurd proposition. I do not deny that to some extent it is true I can be jealous of people who are better off than I am, Harvard professors in particular. Indeed, I would think the fact that all the villagers are in danger of dying this way as a reason for increasing our worry about the matter rather than assuming that the parents don't mind.

To continue with my attack on the relative deprivation hypothesis, I usually refer to it as belief that if everybody has a toothache it doesn't really hurt. I should say that in my opinion this kind of feeling is pre- dominantly an upper class one. We don't worry about starving, but we want to be respected by our acquaintances. This requires that our con- sumption be at least up to community standards. If we were really poor, such matters would be less important. Even if it becomes psycho- logically more important as we become wealthier, and the poor become better off, it is still a secondary effect. The people classified as poor in the United States have many privileges that Louis XIV would have liked.

Let us ignore the lesser cases, and invent a very extreme example. Consider Mr. Jones. He lives in Newport, Rhode Island in the 1890s, and his private yacht is only 100 feet long. None of the people he associates with have private yachts less than 200 feet long. The city fathers feel that this situation of relative deprivation cannot be tolerated. They put a tax on the wealthier people like J. Pierpont Morgan in order to supplement Mr. Jones' income so that he can have a yacht that is 150 feet long. The result of this is greater equality among the yachtsmen of Newport, but the rest of the world as a whole is somewhat worse off if these very highly paid and presumably productive people work less hard in reaction to the tax.[9]

It is hard to argue that this particular equalization of income is a good idea. I should say, however, that I have made this point in a number of lectures. Academia audiences normally showed signs of being unhappy, but did not otherwise respond. On one occasion, however, a professor did point out that in spite of the fact that poor people in the United States and the world were made worse off by this transfer of funds to Mr. Jones for a larger yacht, it might well have been true that the measured inequality of society would decline. This is true, but I have great difficulty believing anyone would support the policy for that reason.

There are, of course, reasons for the sort of behavior that I have been focusing on. Namely, a person may feel more strongly about the poverty of people who live nearby than about the poverty of those living far away. Tucsonites would therefore be more concerned about the poor of Tucson than the poor of Mexico, and no one would be for equalizing American and African incomes. Interestingly, this particular hypothesis would seem to imply that most poverty relief should be initiated at a local level. For instance, the City of Tucson should take care of its poor, with possibly the State of Arizona providing some assistance. But the federal government would be uninvolved in these programs.

It should be said that before the 1930s, aid to the poor was in fact administered locally. Liebergott's studies show that the poor did about as well relatively then as they do now. If people felt more strongly about the poor who are close, they would have done better. So to me, the situation remains a mystery.

A student of mine, studying income tax returns, came to the conclusion that the average American is willing to give about 5 percent of his income to the people who are worse off than he is. This is a rough figure and is only an average. Mother Cabrini gives more than 5 percent, and I am sure there are many people who give less. If you take the amount of money paid out by welfare states to the actual poor, let us define them as the bottom 10 percent, it usually turns out to be about 5 percent of GNP. This is not surprising as, after all, the people who make the private charitable gifts are actually the people who vote for government charitable gifts. So, we get the same outcome in both areas.

These data have led me to a rule of thumb, which is simply that people are willing to give away approximately 5 percent of their incomes for the aid of the poor and downtrodden. The whole thing is rather like dropping a stone into a bottomless pit. No one has ever complained about it. There are people who claim they give much more than 5 percent, but I am a little skeptical in most cases. Yet the fact that some people give more than 5 percent is not surprising. There are also people who seem to think that any government transfer even if it goes to millionaire farmers is somehow a charitable gift. Although no one ever objects to my generalization, I am impressed by the fact that it is rare anyone even comments on it. Further, with one exception, no one ever cites this particular point of view.[10] Note, I am not saying that people refuse to believe. They never object to it. It is just something that is dropped into the memory hole.

If we move from the amount of money that people actually give away to what people say, they would appear to be much more charitable than they actually are. Thus, the American government is accused of being heartless because it doesn't give even more money to the poor. Frequently moralists accuse the whole society of being unduly selfish. It is noteworthy then that in the 1980s—supposedly the decade of indulgence, selfishness, and greed—private contributions to charity rose more rapidly than in any other recent decade. The people who decry the zeitgeist of selfishness never mention this.

I take a radically different attitude from most people. I observe people saying that they are more charitable than they actually are, and criticizing other people for not being more charitable than they actually are. The normal reaction is that we should all be nicer. My reaction is different. I think we should simply admit that we are all charitable, but not very much so. Since we don't seem to be able to get these charitable contributions up above 5 percent, I would suggest that we simply admit this fact, and change what we say rather than what we do.

Economists normally think that what people do is a better measure of their preferences than what they say. Democratic governments are designed to give people what they want. By this is meant what they actually want, not what people say they want. I can think of all sorts of changes in the behavior of most groups which I think would be a good idea. We live in a democracy and democracies do what most people want, not what I want. I can vote like anyone else if I want to use it. Engaging in moral lectures on what people should want is a harmless activity, but it is also an unproductive one. Everyone is in favor of helping the poor, at least a little bit. However, there is little discussion of the theoretical problems surrounding income transfers. I hope that these realities regarding the motivation for and effect of redistribution would be carefully considered before any drastic antipoverty measures are taken.

NOTES

1. I am ignoring the point that was made by Browning and reinforced by other people that the transfer actually costs much more than the benefit. The reason is that it changes the behavior of both the victims and the people to whom it would be transferred. It is not that I regard this as wrong or unimportant, but it is not necessary for this discussion.

2. Plus the top 80 percent.

3. Probably the best presentation of this point of view was by Stephen Marglin, "The Social Rate of Discount and the Optimal Rate of Investment" in *Quarterly Journal of Economics*, February 1963, pp. 95-111. This argument was replied to by me in "The Social Rate of Discount and the Optimal Rate of Investment: Comment" in *Quarterly Journal of Economics*, 1968, 58 (4), pp. 788-802. Marglin was also attacked by three other economists. In fact, I think you can say that intellectually it is perhaps the most thoroughly demolished idea in the literature. Nevertheless, the development economists held fast, and Marglin never formally changed position.

4. I trust the reader does not take this suggestion seriously enough so that I will be asked to explain what you do with those poor who literally die of starvation if they have to pay a tax. As a matter of fact, one could designate this a true negative income tax, not the fake negative income tax of the University of Chicago. In this case the tax you paid would be under a certain income proportional to the degree you fell short of that income, and if you are above that certain income you would receive a supplement proportional to the degree you are above. It must be admitted that this scheme deserves the title "Negative Income Tax" better than the more traditional usage.

5. This is famous because of the expense of the bridge. It should be said that like most World Bank projects it was well engineered. You can feel confident that the bridge will not fall down, which is not necessarily true of the work of many of the other aid agencies.

6. I follow the normal nationalistic assumptions and consider only Americans. Most people in the top 80 percent of most countries would be in the bottom 20 percent of ours.

7. James M. Buchanan and Gordon Tullock, *The Calculus of Consent: Logical Foundations of Constitutional Democracy*, Ann Arbor: University of Michigan Press, 1962, pp. 189-201.

8. *The Economics of Income Redistribution*, Dordrecht: Kluwer, 1983.

9. Few of the wealthy people at that time inherited their money.

10. Martin Paldam is that exception.

AUTHOR INDEX

SUBJECT INDEX

About the Institute

The W.E. Upjohn Institute for Employment Research is a nonprofit research organization devoted to finding and promoting solutions to employment-related problems at the national, state, and local level. It is an activity of the W.E. Upjohn Unemployment Trustee Corporation, which was established in 1932 to administer a fund set aside by the late Dr. W.E. Upjohn, founder of The Upjohn Company, to seek ways to counteract the loss of employment income during economic downturns.

The Institute is funded largely by income from the W.E. Upjohn Unemployment Trust, supplemented by outside grants, contracts, and sales of publications. Activities of the Institute comprise the following elements: (1) a research program conducted by a resident staff of professional social scientists; (2) a competitive grant program, which expands and complements the internal research program by providing financial support to researchers outside the Institute; (3) a publications program, which provides the major vehicle for the dissemination of research by staff and grantees, as well as for other selected work in the field; and (4) an Employment Management Services division, which manages most of the publicly funded employment and training programs in the local area.

The broad objectives of the Institute's research, grant, and publication programs are to (1) promote scholarship and experimentation on issues of public and private employment and unemployment policy; and (2) make knowledge and scholarship relevant and useful to policymakers in their pursuit of solutions to employment and unemployment problems.

Current areas of concentration for these programs include causes, consequences, and measures to alleviate unemployment; social insurance and income maintenance programs; compensation; workforce quality; work arrangements; family labor issues; labor-management relations; and regional economic development and local labor markets.